AMERICAN ORIENTAL SERIES

ESSAY 8

THE CANAANITE GOD REŠEP

AMERICAN ORIENTAL SERIES

AMERICAN ORIENTAL SOCIETY
NEW HAVEN, CONNECTICUT
1976

THE CANAANITE GOD REŠEP

BY

WILLIAM J. FULCO, S.J.

AMERICAN ORIENTAL SOCIETY
NEW HAVEN, CONNECTICUT
1976

Second Printing 1986

PHOTOLITHOPRINTED BY CUSHING-MALLOY, INC.
ANN ARBOR, MICHIGAN, UNITED STATES OF AMERICA

TABLE OF CONTENTS

FORWARD

Chapter

I. EGYPTIAN EVIDENCE

A. Introduction. 1

B. Egyptian Material 2

C. Gods Associated with Rešep. 23

D. Rešep's Weapons 28

E. Rešep and the Gazelle 29

F. Rešep in Egypt: Brief Résumé. 30

II. SEMITIC EVIDENCE

A. Onomastica. 33

B. Rešep in Ugaritic Texts 36

C. Phoenician and Aramaic Inscriptions 44

D. Rešep in Carthage, Byblos 54

E. Rešep in the Old Testament. 56

III. CONCLUSION AND SUMMARY

A. Rešep's Name. 63

B. Rešep's Iconography 65

C. Rešep's Egyptian Epithets 67

D. Rešep in Egypt: Themes. 68

E. Rešep in Northwest Semitic Material 69

FORWARD

Surely one of the major preoccupations of Near Eastern scholars for the next many years will be the interpretation of the incredibly rich corpus of tablets from Ebla = Tell Mardikh in Syria. The first published overview of this late Third Millenium, B.C., material (Pettinato in *Or* 44/3 [1975], 361-374) already indicates that there will be an abundance of new material bearing on ancient Semitic deities.

Happily one of the gods mentioned at Ebla is Rešep; so far there is the proper name *eb-du-^{d}Ra-sa-ap* (*Or* 44, 370), but there is better Rešep material to come.

The literary finds from Ebla make it doubly imperative that every effort be made to consolidate and synthesize the pre-Eblaite material to date that deals with the gods of the Near East--where this is possible--in order to provide a firm context in which to situate the new evidence.

Chapter I: Egyptian Evidence

A. INTRODUCTION

A surprising number of monographs on the Canaanite god Rešep have appeared in recent years.[1] On the occasion of presenting two hitherto unpublished Rešep stelae, Cairo 2792 (E18 below) and U Penn E-13620 (E30),[2] I would like to take the opportunity to bring together in one place as complete a catalog as possible of all the ancient material relating to Rešep, to annotate significant secondary source material, and finally, to offer my own critical remarks on various viewpoints and conclusions expressed in recent publications,

1 E.g., W. D. van Wijngaarden, "Karakter en Voorstellingswijze van den God Resjef volgens de egyptische vóór-aziatische Monumenten," OMRO 31 (1932), 28-42; B. Grdseloff, Les débuts du culte de Rechef en Égypte (Cairo, 1942); A. Caquot, "Sur quelques démons de l'Ancien Testament: Reshep, Qeteb, Deber," Semitica 6 (1956), 53-68; W. K. Simpson, "Reshep in Egypt," Or 29 (1960), 63-74; P. Matthiae, "Note sul dio siriano Rešef," OrAn 2 (1963), 27-43; F. Vattioni, "Il dio Resheph," AION 15 (1965), 39-74; D. Conrad, "Der Gott Reschef," ZAW 83 (1971), 157-183; a rather bizarre section of E. Zenger, Die Sinaitheophanie: Untersuchungen zum jahwistischen und elohistischen Geschichtswerk (Würzburg, 1971), 129ff., in which Z. attempts to link intimately the cult of Rešep with that of Yahweh; A. van den Branden, "Le Dieu Rešeph et ses épithètes," Parole de l'Orient 2 (1971: Université Saint-Esprit, Kaslik, Liban), 389-416; M. K. Schretter, Alter Orient und Hellas: Fragen der Beeinflussung griechischen Gedankengutes aus altorientalischen Quellen, dargestellt an den Göttern Nergal, Rescheph, Apollon (Innsbruck, 1974). In addition there are many smaller articles dealing with individual stelae and texts. The majority of these will be cited below.

2 I would like to thank William Kelly Simpson of Yale University and the Museum of Fine Arts, Boston, for calling these stelae to my attention and for ceding publication rights to them. I am also grateful to Mr. David O'Connor of the University Museum, the University of Pennsylvania, for confirming permission to publish U Penn E-13620 and for providing me with photographs of both stelae, and to the curators of the Egyptian Museum, Cairo, for permission to publish Cairo 2792. Professor Leonard Lesko of the University of California, Berkeley, provided me with the translation of and critical notes to the inscription on Cairo 2792 which are incorporated into this study.

without needlessly repeating the research already done by others.[3]

Although Rešep's homeland was in the Syrian area, it will be useful to consider the Egyptian material first, since it is only in Egypt that we find iconographic material.

B. EGYPTIAN MATERIAL

About fifty Egyptian stelae, ostraca, papyri, amulets and scarabs pertain directly to Rešep, or have reasonably been claimed to do so. They are here listed in roughly chronological order. Further details may be found in the literature cited in the footnotes.

(E1). Papyrus Brooklyn 35.1446 [= ANET 553], Vs. A9.[4] Probably Thirteenth Dynasty. In a list of servants, mostly Egyptian but some foreign, occurs ʿpr-ršpw, a brewer (ʿfty) who is an Asiatic (ʿꜣm).[5]

3 A more detailed analysis of the Rešep material and a critical review of the secondary literature available to me up until mid-1970 can be found in my doctoral dissertation, The God Rešep, Yale University, Dec 1970, available through University Microfilms, Ann Arbor, Michigan. I have, frankly, changed my views on several issues since then.

4 W. C. Hayes, A Papyrus of the Late Middle Kingdom in the Brooklyn Museum (Brooklyn, 1955), 87, 94; also Simpson, "New Light on the God Reshef," JAOS 73 (1953), 86-89; Albright, "Northwest-Semitic Names in a List of Egyptian Slaves from the Eighteenth Century, B.C.," JAOS 74 (1954), 225; and Simpson, "Reshep in Egypt," Or 29 (1960), 65-66.

5 The ʿpr element occurs in some half-dozen other names in Egyptian sources: ʿpr-ỉr (= ,-El), ʿpr-bʿr-(= -Baʿal) pꜣ šry, ʿpr-dgr (= -Dagan), etc. See Albright, JAOS 74 (1954), 225; he also cites Greek parallels. Simpson, JAOS 73 (1953), 87, notes the Middle Kingdom ʿpr-hḳ. W. Helck, Die Beziehungen Ägyptens zu Vorderasien im 3. und 2. Jahrtausend v. Chr. (Wiesbaden, 1962), also has examples. Hayes and Albright suggest that the ʿpr element is not natively Egyptian, but Semitic. They cite the Akk. epēru, "to foster, feed, nourish," which is found in several Akk. names: Sin-ēpirī, "Sin fosters me," Šamaš-ēpirī, Marduk-ēpirī. (See also comments of Vattioni, AION 15, 29, n.8). Apparently assuming such an equivalence, Wilson (ANET 553) renders ʿpr-ršp as "Rešep nourishes." On the other hand, Simpson (JAOS 73, 87) notes certain names which appear to be purely Egyptian (presumably because of the apparent verbal forms) which contain ʿpr: ʿpr·f in the Old Kingdom, ʿprt nfr in the Middle Kingdom, and ʿprtỉ in the in the Eighteenth Dynasty, as well as ʿEper-Isis in Ptolemaic times. Here he suggests that ʿpr is an Egyptian verb, although possibly cognate with Akk. epēru. In light of Ugaritic ḫpr, "rations (of food or drink)," however, it would seem that the root underlying Akk. epēru, "to feed," and ipru,

(E2). Ostracon, Metropolitan Museum field no. 27057.5 (W. C. Hayes excavation).[6] Thebes, early reign of Amenophis III. Proper name ʿpr-ršpw.

(E3). Sphinx Stele of Amenophis II, Urk. IV 1282:15 [= ANET 224].[7] This stele from Gizeh describes the youthful equestrian and martial prowess of Amenophis II, and he is praised for his likeness to Montu: "He knew every task of Montu; there was none like him on the field of battle. . . .his majesty appeared in a chariot like Montu in his power, . . .shooting at them like Montu in battle." After a passage providing hints for horsemanship from Amenophis' elders, this occurs: "Now after it had been entrusted to the king's son to take care of the horses of the king's stable, -- ỉst rf sw ḥr ỉrt rdyt m ḥr·f ršp ʿstỉrtw hʿ·w ỉm·f ḥr ỉrt mrrt nbt ỉb·f, -- well then he did that which was entrusted to him. Rešep and ʿAstarte were rejoicing in him for all that his heart desired."

Note: Rešep is associated with horsemanship (and indirectly with battle), he is coupled with ʿAstarte, he is associated with Montu. Grdseloff[8] uses this as partial evidence that Rešep was "formally" introduced into Egypt during the reign of Amenophis II.

(E4). Festival Building of Amenophis II at Karnak, Relief at G 235.[9] Damaged relief: parts of horses, horseman, chariot wheel. Broken inscription, part of which is [m]ntw ršp, each name followed by the divine determinative. Montu-Rešep? Montu and Rešep?

(E5). Parallel texts, Memphis (Mit Rahineh) Stele and Thebes (Karnak) Stele, Urk. IV 1302:7/1131:2.[10] Amenophis II. The Memphis version reads: dꜣ·n ḥm·f ỉrntw ḥr mw m hsmḳ [?] mỉ ršp, "His majesty crossed the Orontes over the waters m hsmḳ [?] like Rešep('s)." m hsmḳ is difficult,[11] but the general image is clear. Pharaoh is likened to

---

"food," is not ʿPR but ḪPR, of which ʿpr in Egyptian would not seem to be a possible reflex. Tentatively, then, we must fall back on the attested Egyptian verb, ʿpr, "to provide, to equip," whence: "Rešep provides." See also now J. J. M. Roberts, The Earliest Semitic Pantheon: A Study of the Semitic Deities Attested in Mesopotamia before Ur III (Baltimore, 1972), 63-64, n. 13.

6 Simpson, Or 29 (1960), 66; Albright, JAOS 74 (1954), 225. H. Ranke, Die ägyptischen Personennamen (Glückstadt, 1935), I, 227, lists ršpw as a personal name which he dates to the Middle Kingdom. He inadvertently cites Kminek-Szedlo, Saggio Filologico. It should be K.-S., Catalogo del Museo Civico di Bologna (Turin, 1895), No. 1821.

7 Simpson, Or 29 (1960), 65; Grdseloff, Les débuts, 6; J. Leibovitch, "Quelques nouvelles représentations du dieu Rechef," ASAE 39 (1939), 185; Helck, Beziehungen, 485.

8 Grdseloff, Les débuts, 6.

9 Simpson, Or 29 (1960), 64-65 and Pl. 1 [= Tab. XVII].

10 Helck, Urkunden der 18. Dynastie (Berlin, 1955), XVII.

11 The -m- of hsmḳ is the arm holding the cone. Drioton's argument

Rešep as an awesome warrior out to battle. This interpretation is furthered by the parallel Theban text where for *mỉ ršp* there stands *mỉ pḥty mntw wꜣst*, "like the strength of Theban Montu," Montu being the Theban god of military prowess. The scribal relationship between the parallel versions is not certain,[12] but what is significant is the interchange between Rešep and Montu.

(E6). *Grdseloff Seal Impression of Amenophis II.*[13] A scarab-shaped seal-impression bearing this inscription: *ꜥꜣ-ḫprw-rꜥ mry ršp, "ꜥAḫeperureꜥ [= Amenophis II], beloved of Rešep."* This would seem to indicate that Rešep was a special patron of Amenophis II.

(E7). "*Fish Amulet*" *43, Palace of Amenophis III.*[14] Inscription: *ršpw*. Note spelling with *-w*.

(*ASAE* 45 [1947], 61-64) that this must be read *m* and not *d* seems conclusive, despite the insistence of Grdseloff (*ASAE* 45 [1947], 115-118). Grdseloff's critique of Drioton is elaborate, involving the entire passage, but Edel (*ZDPV* 69 [1963], 140-141) would seem to have effectively laid it to rest. *hsmḳ* is an unknown word. It is followed by 𓂻, so would seem to rule out the early translation cited by Drioton (62): "Darauf überquerte seine Majestät den Orontes zu Wasser, indem er sich durchnässen liess wie Reschef." Drioton suggests either an unknown Afroasiatic root in the Š-stem: *S/ŠMG/Q* or a Hitp. of *MG/Q*, the most likely prospect being *MWG*, the Heb. "to wave, swerve, flow." Assuming that it is the water that is agitated, Drioton translates "Sa majesté traversera l'Oronte sur des eaux en furie, comme Rechef." He suggests that this might refer to the annual inundation. Simpson translates "over tempestuous [?] waters," also making *hsmḳ* modify *mw*. I would offer that the word order tolerates another interpretation: "His majesty crossed the Orontes over the waters, --with *hsmḳ* (disturbance? violence?) like Rešep's." Cf. Helck's "Königlichen Stelen sprechen vom Pharao, dass er 'wie Reschef durch die Furt des Orontes hindurchstürmt.'"

12 Drioton (*ASAE* 45 [1947], 61-62) suggests that the original version of the text is the Memphitic with Rešep, and that Montu was substituted in Thebes because he was not thought of as having rivals in matters martial. Grdseloff (*ASAE* 45 [1947], 117-118) proposes that there has been a re-engraving of the Memphis stele: originally it read *mntw*, but was changed to *ršp* after the Amarna period. Edel (*ZDPV* 69 [1963], 140-141) suggests roughly the opposite. As Simpson (*Or* 29 [1960], 65, n.3) indicates, however, Helck in the *Urkunden* indicates no traces of restoration on either stele. Simpson's own comment: "This interchange of Montu and Rešep may indicate that Rešep was felt to be closest to Montu among the native Egyptian gods."

13 Grdseloff, *Les débuts*, 1-2 and Pl. 1. Grdseloff purchased the impression in Cairo, does not question its authenticity.

14 W. C. Hayes, "Inscriptions from the Palace of Amenophis III," *JNES* 10 (1951), 234 and fig. R43; Simpson, *Or* 29 (1960), 66, and *BMMA* 10:6 (1952), Pl. on 187.

(E8). Graffito of Gebel Agg [Tôškeh], Nubia.[15] Probably Eighteenth Dynasty. Rešep in high conical hat, holding mace[16] over his head and a shield. He is labeled ršp (spelled r-šp, 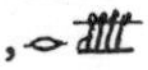, which is unique) nṯr ʿȝ nb pt, "Rešep, the great god, lord of the sky." He is possibly to be associated with one of the five offerers, who carries a bow, arrows and a gazelle.[17]

(E9). Stele Berlin 14462.[18] Probably Theban, Eighteenth Dynasty. Rešep stands holding an "apple" mace over his head with his right hand, a shield and a spear in his left. Uraeus on Upper Egyptian crown. ršp nṯr ʿȝ sḏm nḥ, "Rešep, the great god, who hears prayer."

(E10). Stele Cairo 70222.[19] Unknown provenance. Eighteenth Dynasty?[20] A votive stele of ỉmn-m-ỉpt. Rešep (ršp nṯr ʿȝ) wears a short kilt, upper garment, collar and Upper Egyptian crown with tasseled cords in back and a gazelle-head in front. He brandishes a mace-axe in his right hand, a shield in his left. A stylized sunshade is behind him.

(E11). Sai Relief, S. 108.[21] Eighteenth Dynasty. A fragment with the head of a horse facing right into the fragment. The shield of a rider is still visible. There is a broken inscription in three

15 A. Weigall, A Report on the Antiquities of Lower Nubia and Their Condition in 1906-07 (Oxford, 1907), 124-125 and Pl. LXVI; Leibovitch, ASAE 39 (1939), 156ff. and Pl. XIX, 2; Grdseloff, Les débuts, 11ff. most recently (and most thoroughly), Simpson, Heka-nefer and the Dynastic Material from Toshka and Arminna (New Haven, 1963), 36-38 and fig. 32.

16 Simpson's drawing has it look like a spear, but the photograph in Leibovitch suggests rather a mace.

17 On the left half of the graffito are five offerers, all walking to the right, bearing gifts. They are, left to right, a male carrying two boomerangs (?); a male carrying a pair of sandals and a bird; a male carrying a bow, arrows and a (slain?) gazelle; a female with a conical bread loaf; and a male offering incense and pouring a libation on an altar. Seated facing the offerers are Horus of Maʿam, Sesostris III with a lotus before him, and Rešep. The offerings of the third male are all things associated with Rešep. Sesostris III, Twelfth Dynasty, was deified and worshipped through Nubia in the Eighteenth Dynasty.

18 Published in separate fragments: Spiegelberg, OLZ 12 (1908), 529 and Pl. 1; Grdseloff, Les débuts, 7-11 and Pl. LL. See also Leibovitch, ASAE 39 (1939), 147-148.

19 Leibovitch, ASAE 39 (1939), 148-154; Grdseloff, Les débuts, 8.

20 Because of the wḥm ʿnḫ, "live again," following the name of the offerer, Grdseloff (8, n.2) dates this stele to the Eighteenth dynasty when the expression was in vogue.

21 J. Vercoutter, "Excavations at Sai 1955-57," Kush 6 (1958), 155-156 and Pl. XLVa.

columns which reads:[22] *mꜣꜣ ḫrw[y]* / *ntb sw šnw bw* [with traces of  here?] / *ršp*, perhaps to be translated "When an enemy is seen, the encircler [of the desert], Rešep scorches him." The presumption is that Rešep was the rider on this relief.[23]

(E12). *Abusir Relief, Berlin 19808.*[24] Only forepart of figure extant on fragment, head to waist. The left hand holds a spear and a shield; the right hand near the waist seems to be holding reins. Leclant[25] translates the broken inscription "[Je te donne] toute contrée étrangère sous tes sandales." L. Burchardt[26] believes the figure is Rešep, as does Helck.[27] Leclant[28] argues that it is ʿAstarte. It could even be ʿAnat. Unfortunately there is just not enough of the relief left to make a definitive judgment.

(E13). *Aberdeen Stele.*[29] Possibly Eighteenth Dynasty.[30] On this votive stele Rešep strides to the right, a mace-axe over his head in his right hand, a shield in his left. He wears an Upper Egyptian crown. There appear to be traces of a hanging ribbon from the back of

22 I owe this suggested translation again to Leonard Lesko. Vercoutter does not attempt a translation, but gives a hieroglyphic reading identical to Lesko's except that for the oar-sign of *ḫrwy* he reads a *nfr*-sign.

23 Leclant, *Syria* 37 (1960), 29-30, argues for ʿAstarte, despite the inscription. See R. Stadelmann, *Syrisch-palästinensische Gottheiten in Ägypten* (Leiden, 1967) [hereafter *Gottheiten*], 57, where he compares the iconography of Rešep with that of ʿAstarte.

24 L. Burchardt, *Das Grabdenkmal des Königs Saꜣḥu-reʿ* (Leipzig, 1910), I, 126; Leclant, *Syria* 37 (1960), 28-29 and fig. 8.

25 Leclant, *Syria* 37 (1960), 29.

26 Burchardt, *Das Grabdenkmal*, I, 126.

27 Helck, *Beziehungen*, 486.

28 Leclant, *Syria* 37 (1960), 29.

29 First publication, Spiegelberg, *ZfA* 20 (1898), 120ff.

30 Griffith (*PSBA* 22 [1900], 171-172), following Spiegelberg (apparently a private communication from S. to G.) dates the stele to the Twentieth or perhaps Twenty-First Dynasty, although he offers no arguments. There are certain parallels between the Aberdeen stele and *Stele Cairo 70222* (E10) which is dated to the Eighteenth Dynasty. See Leibovitch, *ASAE* 39 (1939), 151ff. Goossens (*ChrE* 29 [1940], 65-66) ventures no dating. de Meulenaere ("De cultus van Resjef in Egypte," *Handelingen van het Eentwintigste Vlaams Filologencongres* [Leuven, 1955], 129-131) says the name of the votive offerer as well as individual orthographic and paleographic peculiarities strongly suggest that the stele dates from the beginning of the Eighteenth Dynasty, certainly before Amenophis II, and was manufactured in Memphis. If so, this would make it the oldest iconographic item from Egypt of Rešep. de Meulenaere does not detail his argument.

the crown. Behind Rešep is a sun-shade. Facing him is an offerer, ỉʿhmss, and there is a table of offerings between them.

Rešep is identified as ršp šꜣrmʿnꜣ, Rešep-Šulman, about whom we shall deal later. The divine determinative follows each member of the compound name (recall mntw-ršp in E4), and the whole is determined by the "foreigner" boomerang sign.

(E14.) Cassirer Scarab.[31] Fine steatite, probably mid-Eighteenth Dynasty. The figure on this scarab wears a high Upper Egyptian crown with what may be a gazelle-head in front. There is a tassel down the back of the crown. There is no indication of any body garment. What is unlike expected Rešep-iconography is that he has wings, and his crown is surmounted by a solar disk. He is occupied with slaying an immense serpent.

Cassirer unhesitatingly names this figure Rešep. Leibovitch[32] publishes another scarab with a similar divinity: he is riding on the back of an animal (a lion?), has wings or fringed arms, but instead of a gazelle-head (if, indeed, that is what is on the Cassirer scarab), he has horns.

What may be the same horned deity, again on an animal (lion?), but this time without wings, occurs on a scarab published by Rowe[33] and cited by Leibovitch.[34] As Leibovitch well demonstrates, these horns can readily be associated with deities other than Rešep.[35]

The safest hypothesis is that all three of these scarabs depict the same unidentified deity who most likely is not Rešep--or it is possible that one or other of the scarabs has this unknown deity at its base, but has become contaminated by artistic freedom or religious syncretism.

(E15). Scarab Jerusalem 574 [32.2672].[36] Unknown provenance. Rowe dates to Eighteenth Dynasty. The god on the scarab looks indeed like Rešep: he wears a high conical crown, carries a weapon in his uplifted right hand, a shield in his left.[37]

31 M. Cassirer, "A Scarab with an Early Representation of Resheph," JEA 45 (1959), 6-7 and Pls. 16, 1c.

32 Leibovitch, ASAE 42 (1942), 441, fig. 90. He does not know its provenance. For further examples and a lengthy discussion, see Leclant, Syria 37 (1960), 62-67.

33 A. Rowe, A Catalogue of Egyptian Scarabs, Scaraboids, Seals and Amulets in the Palestine Archaeological Museum (Cairo, 1936), No.722 [32.1580] and Pl. XVIII.

34 Leibovitch, ASAE 42 (1942), 441, fig 91.

35 See figs. 81-89 in Leibovitch, ASAE 42 (1942), 438-441.

36 Rowe, Scarabs, 138 and Pl. XV.

37 Rowe says he holds a uraeus, but I believe it is a shield, seen from the side, and that the uraeus is in the field above it, just as the nfr-sign behind him and the branch before him.

(E16). Seal Jerusalem 57 [34.3123].[38] From Tell ed-Duweir. Rowe dates to the Eighteenth Dynasty. Rowe's photograph is not very clear. His description: "To the left is a figure of the Canaanite god Resheph holding a battle axe in his left hand and a shield in his right. He is adorned in a kilt and wears a conical crown (with a gazelle's head [?] attached). In front of the god is a small conventional tree, and behind him a quiver (?). To the right is a large conventional tree with branches ending in concentric circles."

(E17). Portion of Stele BM 478 [264].[39] Probably from Thebes, Nineteenth Dynasty. A fairly typical sepulchral stele. Rešep (here ršpw) unfortunately does not appear on this fragment, but undoubtedly appeared in the lost upper register. The offerer, pꜣ-šd, is shown in a position of supplication, invoking Rešep with prayers for life, health and strength, in a text similar to Cairo 2792.

(E18). Stele Cairo 2792 [hitherto unpublished].[40] (Plate I, figure 1). Probably Memphis, late Nineteenth Dynasty. Limestone, 430 cm. wide, 672 cm. high, badly abraded, especially across center of upper register.

Rešep is depicted as striding to the right, brandishing what seems to be a pole-axe over his head in his right hand. His left hand holds a spear (the shaft is discernible), and--if I am not reading into the traces I see--a shield. At the top of the upper register in two columns is ršp nṯr ʿꜣ nb pt, "Rešep, the great god, lord of the sky." Before Rešep is an offering table heaped with offerings.

In the lower register a man kneels on the right facing left, his hands raised in supplication. Before him are heaps of offerings. To the far left is an inscription in four columns:[41]

38 Rowe, Scarabs, 250 and Pl. XXVII.

39 British Museum: A Guidebook to the Egyptian Galleries (Sculpture) (London, 1909), 135 [hereafter Guidebook]; H. R. Hall, Hieroglyphic Texts from Egyptian Stelae, etc., in the British Museum (London, 1925), VII, Pl. 41/2. See also remarks on E37 Below.

40 From the find register of the Cairo Museum: "Badly weathered, found below water level with three others in situ in south wall of a room west of the great south portal of Merenptah."

41 Translation and notes on translation by Leonard Lesko.

[a]The first sign is clearly [hieroglyph], and we would expect the tall sign below it to the left to be Δ. Instead there seems to be either [hieroglyph] or [hieroglyph]. Similar miswritings with both these signs are known. For [hieroglyph] cf. B.M. Stele 989 in I. E. Edwards, Hieroglyphic Texts from Egyptian Stelae, etc. (London, 1939), VIII, Pl. XLVI. For [hieroglyph] cf. B.M. Stele 211 in Hall, Hieroglyphic Texts, etc., VII, Pl. 35.

[b]Certainly a carelessly carved [hieroglyph]. For a similar dỉ·ỉ ỉꜣw n pꜣy·t ḥr nfr, cf. J. Černý, Egyptian Stelae in the Bankes Collection (Oxford, 1958), No. 7.

[c]These two first-person singular suffixes are uncertain, but seem very likely, based on the available space and context. Most often either an agent expression or a purpose clause in the third person (referring to the

"Giving[a] praise to Rešep, kissing the ground to his ka. It is to his beautiful[b] face that I[c] give praise, so that I[c] may propitiate his goodness. You heal[d] [my] arms and ⌈open⌉[e] my eyes [with][f] the sight of your face, ⌈for the ka of the scribe⌉ Peqrer.[g]"

(E19). Stele Cairo 86123.[42] Probably from the Delta, Qantir, and Nineteenth Dynasty.[43] This stele has two registers. In the upper register, both facing left, are Amon-Reʿ (ỉmn-rʿ nsw nṯrw, "Amon-Reʿ, king of the gods") and Rešep (simply ršpw). In front of them is an offering table and a large lotus. Both gods carry wꜣs-scepters in their right hand, ʿankhs in their left. Rešep's conical crown has a gazelle-head in front, two ribbons in back. He wears a short kilt.

In the lower register is Ḥoron (ḥwrwn), also with wꜣs and ʿankh. The worshipper before him has a name compounded with ṯnr (= ṯl?) with a boomerang determinative, indicating he is a foreigner. Ḥoron seems to have been assimilated into the Egyptian pantheon under Amenophis II.

(E20). Seal Jerusalem 60A [35.4442] [= ANEP 468].[44] From Bethel, probably Nineteenth Dynasty. Two figures face each other on this cylinder seal, and between them is a panel with hieroglyphic ʿštrt. The figure on the right, which seems surely to be ʿAstarte, is dressed in a long tunic and carries a spear in her right hand. Rowe suggests that she might be carrying an ʿankh in her left hand, but I am not able to

god) follows rdỉ ỉꜣw. . ., but another example with the first person dỉ·ỉ occurs in B.M. Stele 812. Cf. Hall, Hieroglyphic Texts, VII, Pl. 26

[d]Because of the spacing I have decided to read snb with a short, straight — over , rather than swꜣb with which could be argued.

[e]This mostly a guess based on the context and determinative. I cannot really see wn or mḥ in the surviving traces and I am tempted to suggest ꜣwỉ, "extend," related to ꜣw, "wide," which is well known for its use with "eyes" in Coptic.

[f]There is room for a sign or signs at the top of this line. Based on what looks like a horizontal line at the bottom of this space, I suggest reading .

[g]The end of the petitioner's name is unclear, but I have decided to keep a second rather than either a fish as in (Wb. I, 500, 5) or as in (Wien Stele: cf. J. D. C. Lieblein, Dictionnaire de noms hiéroglyphiques en ordre généalogique et alphebêtique (I: Christiana, 1871 and II: Leipzig, 1892), 743, No. 1907; E. von Bergmann, "Inschriftliche Denkmäler," in Recueil de Travaux 12 (1892), 14.

42 Leibovitch, "Amon-raʿ, Rechef et Ḥouroun sue une stèle," ASAE 44 (1944), 163-172; Habachi, "Khatâʿna-Qantîr: Importance," ASAE 52 (1954), 443-462 with Plates.

43 Leibovitch places the stele in the Eighteenth or Nineteenth Dynasty, suggesting the reign of Ramses II or Ramses III as most likely, largely because of the costuming, general appearance, and because ŝʿšꜣ (not otherwise attested until after the Eighteenth Dynasty) and ṯnr, usually associated with the Nineteenth Dynasty, occur in the lower register.

44 Rowe, Scarabs, 251-252.

Fig. 1: E18, Stele Cairo 2792

detect it.

The figure to the left wears a conical but flattened hat with two horns. He/she wears a short kilt, brandishes a harpê in the right hand and holds a spear in the left. There has been speculation that this is Rešep,[45] Seth, or even Rešep-Seth. I am not at all convinced that this is Rešep, and suspect it may even be another ʿAstarte.

45 See discussion in Rowe, Scarabs, 252, and in Leibovitch, ASAE 42 (1942), 438-441, re Seth and horns. Cf. E14.

(E21). Chester Beatty Papyrus VII, Vs 4:9.[46] Time of Ramses II. Rešep (here ršpw) appears in a list of gods who protect various parts of the body. The text is a warning to a particular poison:

"Thou shalt not take thy stand in his hindquarters,
Hathor is against thee, lady of the hindquarters.
Thou shalt not take thy stand in his phallus,
Horus is against thee, lord of the phallus.
Thou shalt not take up thy stand in his ꜣst,
Rešep is against thee, lord of the ꜣst."

ꜣst is an unknown term. The progression is: back, internal organs, hindquarters, phallus, ꜣst, thighs, knee, shin, feet. One would expect, then, something in the area of the genitals for ꜣst, and if specifically genital, certainly male.[47] The association of specific gods with various parts of the body seems arbitrary.[48]

(E22). Leibovitch Fragment.[49] Possibly Theban, probably time of Ramses II. Rešep is not mentioned on this fragment, but the iconography is unmistakable. The figure strides right with his right arm over his head, surely brandishing a weapon (section missing). His left hand is in front of him, probably holding a spear, shield or both. He wears an Upper Egyptian crown with two ribbons down the back. The front of the crown is abraded. There is a quiver on his back, and from his right arm hangs a lute-like instrument which we will also encounter on E23 and E24. The extant inscription is ỉr n sš st mꜥꜣt r[ꜥ-]mss, "Made by the scribe of the Theban necropolis, rꜥ-mss."

(E23). Temple of Ptah Stele.[50] From Memphis, probably time of Ramses II. This is a votive stele of a certain [. . .ḥ]tp. The offerer kneels before Rešep and an offering table. Rešep strides right, brandishing a simple mace over his head with his right hand. In his left hand he holds a shield. There is the usual conical crown, but with a uraeus in front instead of a gazelle-head. There are no ribbons. Behind Rešep is a lute-like instrument similar to that on E22. To the rear and above is rdỉ ꜥnḫ nfr, "giving good life," [r]šp nṯr ꜥꜣ, and remnants of the principal inscription.

(E24). Stele Hildesheim 1100.[51] From Qantir, Ramesside. Rešep

46 A. H. Gardiner, Hieratic Papyri in the British Museum: Third Series, Chester Beatty Gift (London, 1935), I, 64. See also Simpson, Or 29 (1960), 67.

47 Gardiner's suggestion of "marrow" seems quite unlikely, and even more so is Helck's "Gebärmutter"! (Beziehungen, 485).

48 For an excellent, though brief, study of this type of association in Egyptian texts, see A. Massart, The Leiden Magical Papyrus I 343 + I 345 [= Sup. to OMRO 34] (Leiden, 1954), 88.

49 Leibovitch, "Une fragment de stèle dédiée à Rechef," ASAE 40 (1940), 489-492.

50 F. Petrie, Meydum and Memphis III (London, 1910), 39 and Pl. XXXIV, 5. Also Leibovitch, ASAE 40 (1940), 490.

51 L. Habachi, ASAE 52 (1954), 513-514 and esp. 541; also Leibovitch, ASAE 40 (1940), 490ff., and Simpson Or 29 (1960), 71.

stands facing right, wearing an Upper Egyptian crown, two tassels down the back. He brandishes a spear in his right hand, holds a spear and shield in his left. Behind him once more is a lute-like instrument.[52] Legible parts of the inscription are ršpw nṯr ʿ3 and ḥtp dỉ nsw. Habachi also reads sḏm nḥ(wt), but I am unable to do so.

(E25). Stele BM 647 [263].[53] Thebes, Nineteenth Dynasty. This stele is listed in the British Museum catalog as follows: "Limestone sepulchral stele with rounded top, on which is cut the figure of the god Reshpu [ršpw] who wears the White Crown with bandlet, and a tunic reaching to his knees, and holds a mace in his right hand, and a spear and buckler in the left. Before him is a table of offerings. The name of the deceased is not given. Belmore Col[lection]."

(E26). Leiden Magical Papyrus I 343 + I 345, R/Vs 6-7 & R/Rt XI: 13-14.[54] Probably late Nineteenth Dynasty. This magical papyrus invokes the "poisons" of several gods against what is apparently a disease, s3mwn3, evidently a foreign word. After mentioning "the god above (nṯr ḥry) and his wife Ningal (nwk3r), the text continues: n3 n mtwt n ršpw ḥnʿ ỉtwm t3y·f ḥmt, "the poisons of Rešep and his wife Itom." Itom cannot be identified with certainty.[55]

52 Variations of this instrument are found on E22, E23 and E24. In each case the instrument has double cords or thongs at its end. On E22 it is suspended from Rešep's uplifted right arm. It is marked with two holes or spots on the main body, much like the hieroglyphic ink-palette. On E23 the instrument is suspended from Rešep's waist. The handle protrudes into the oval section like an oar. The instrument, this time with its oval section looking somewhat like a donut, is placed behind Rešep as a symbol. Leibovitch (ASAE 48 [1948], 498-492) has made great efforts to identify the object, but concludes only that it surely is not a musical instrument, and that if it is a weapon, it is impossible to guess its function. He likens it to unidentified objects (492, fig. 62) found sometimes on the friezes of Middle Egyptian tombs, which look like painted gourds. I believe the length of the handles, the tassels, and the general appearance of the Rešep-instruments makes this identification unlikely. Glancing through various paintings of Egyptian lutes, I am convinced that Rešep's instrument is indeed a lute. Cf. A. Mekhitarian, Egyptian Painting [SKIRA Series] (Geneva, 1954), 33, "Women musicians, Tomb of Nakht; G. Posener, A Dictionary of Egyptian Civilization (London, 1962), 179, Plates; Noblecourt and Yoyotte, Treasures of the Pharaohs [SKIRA Series] (Geneva, 1968), 92: faience bowl with girl playing lute. The only explanation I can offer is that the lute is an Asian instrument, and was perhaps a symbol of Rešep Asian origin? I see nothing in the history of Egyptian music which would suggest an intrinsic relationship between the lute and Rešep.

53 British Museum, Guidebook (1909), 180.

54 A. Massart, Leiden Papyrus (cf. note 48 above), 17 and 65; Simpson, Or 29 (1960), 68; Gardiner, "The Goddess Ningal in an Egyptian Text," note in ZÄS 43 (1906), 97; Grdseloff, Le dêbuts, 25.

55 Grdseloff (Les dêbuts, 25), following N. Burchardt (Die altkanaanäischen Fremdworte und Eigennamen in Ägyptischen [Leipsiz, 1909], II, 10,

In Rt XI:13-14, against what is also apparently a disease, ʿḫw, we find this line in a very broken context: ỉỉ·k ḫft nꜣ nty ršpw ḥr ḥdb, "You shall go before those whom Rešep kills." Both in this instance and in the one preceding, Rešep is associated with disease and possibly death, but evidently in a positive, protective connection.[56]

(E27). Cambridge Stele, Fitzwilliam Museum.[57] Possibly from Deir el Medineh, Nineteenth Dynasty.[58] On the upper register of this votive stele Rešep sits facing right. His usual Upper Egyptian crown has a gazelle-head in front. He holds a mace in his right hand, a shield in his left. Behind him is a large ʿankh with arms holding a flabellum. Above this symbol is sꜣ ʿnḫ hꜣ·f, "Protection of life is around him." Distributed on either side of the shield is ršpw nṯr ʿꜣ.

On the lower panel are two worshippers to the right, facing left, with this inscription: rdỉ ỉꜣw(t) n ršpw nṯr ʿꜣ dỉ·f wḏꜣ snb n kꜣ n sḏm-ʿš n st mʿꜣt pꜣ-šd, "Giving homage to Rešep, the great god, that he may give life, prosperity and health to the ka of his servant in the Theban necropolis, pꜣ-šd."

(E28). Stele, Calvet Museum (Avignon) 16.[59] Probably Nineteenth Dynasty and from Deir el Medineh. Rešep (ršpw nṯr ʿꜣ) sits with a mace-axe over his head, shield in the left hand before him, Upper Egyptian crown with tassels and a gazelle-head.[60]

No. 117) sees ỉtwm = ʿdwm = Edom. He posits an original compound name Šamaš-Atum/Edom, "the Red Sun." (As a place name, see Gardiner, Egypt of the Pharaohs [Oxford, 1964], 201). Massart (Leiden Papyrus, 68), suggests that whereas Šapš is a feminine deity in Northwest Semitic (e.g., Ugaritic), the scribe of this magical text comes to refer to ỉtwm as Rešep's consort. Both Massart and Grdseloff cite the proper name ỉtmỉby, "Edom is my father (?)," in their arguments. Cf. G. Posener, Princes et pays d'Asie et de Nubie (Brussels, 1940), 64.

56 It is likely that in this as well as in other magical texts, there is a tendency for the scribe to invoke appropriately exotic deities. For this reason it is difficult to assess how closely gods should be associated with the functions they are assigned in such texts. Often their names are invoked simply for their pun-value. (Incidentally, the name of ʿAnat--ʿntỉ--occurs in R VI:1.)

57 J. M. A. Janssen, "Une stèle du dieu Reshef à Cambridge," ChrE 50 (1950), 209-212.

58 Because of the obvious relationships between this stele and the pꜣ-šd stele (E17), Janssen would date it to the Nineteenth Dynasty, as he does E17. See his discussion, ChrE 50, 211-213.

59 Leclant, "Astarté à cheval d'après les représentations egyptiennes," Syria 37 (1960), 27.

60 May I suggest a sip or two of brandy before reading this footnote? J. G. Wilkinson, The Manners and Customs of the Ancient Egyptians (Originally London, 1840; rev. by S. Birch: London, 1878), III, Pl. LV center, opposite p. 234, published a line drawing of Rešep without identifying the stele from which he adapted it. Wijngaarden, OMRO 10 (1932), 33, fig. 21b,

(E29). Stele, Oriental Institute, Chicago, 10569 [= ANEP 476].[61] Possibly from Deir el Medineh, and probably Ramesside. On this stele Rešep strides to the right. He wears the crown of Upper Egypt with a gazelle-head in front, and from the top, two ribbons flow down his back. His kilt, affixed from the shoulder with crossed chest-bands,[62] is elaborately tasseled at the bottom, typically Asiatic in appearance.[63] An unidentified object (an animal tail? a small version of our "lute"?) hangs with tassels from his right arm, which arm brandishes a fenestrated axe. In his left hand is a spear and a shield.[64]

My reading of the inscription to the right is ršpw ḳꜣb·f nṯr ʿꜣ di͗·f n·k ʿnḫ snb rʿ nb. Simpson[65] translates "Reshpu, he who winds about [ḳꜣb], the great god; may he give you all life and health every day." Of ḳꜣb as "wind about" Simpson says, "The phrase. . .is rather curious and might refer to lightening or to the storm god quickly turning about to smite his enemy." Despite what has often been said, however, which will be discussed later, there is little to recommend the idea that Rešep is a storm god. Somewhat preferable is Helck's[66] suggestion, "der vermehrt," certainly a legitimate handling of ḳꜣb. A more hazardous--but certainly attractive--hypothesis is that ḳꜣb represents Semitic QRB, and that ršpw ḳꜣb·f is "Rešep who draws near

---

reproduced the picture but also did not recognize the source of Wilkinson's figure. Jansse, ChrE 50 (1950), 211-212 and 212 note, writing in 1950 about the Cambridge stele reported that he had been told that BM 647 [263] (here E25) was the one illustrated in Wilkinson, although he was not able to obtain W.'s book to verify it. Now it so happens that Wilkinson's figure is identical to the Calvet stele (E28), a photograph of which appears in Leclant, Syria 37 (1960), 27, fig. 7. But since it is also very much like the photograph of the Cambridge stele, and certainly fits the description of BM 647, it's a toss-up as to what Wilkinson actually had before him. I'm not too sure anyone really cares, but it has de facto complicated the secondary literature. (On the Cambridge stele, the mace-axe is held farther back and at a greater angle.)

61 Published fully by Simpson, "An Egyptian Statuette of a Phoenician God," BMMA 10:6 (1952), 184 and Pl. on 185.

62 For crossed chest-bands on this stele and in general, see M. Pope, "The Saltier of Atargatis Reconsidered," Near Eastern Archaeology in the Twentieth Century: Essays in Honor of Nelson Glueck (Garden City, N.Y., 1970), 178-196.

63 See, for example, the tomb painting of Seti I where the "four races" are depicted: Rachewiltz (Sadea/Sansoni, ed.), La Valle dei Re e delle Regine [= Forme e Colore, No. 37] (Firenze, 1965), Folio intro. cols 7,8.

64 To the left on the stele is the name of its dedicator: "For the ka of the priest of Ḥorus-Khenty-Eẖtay, Lord of Athribis, Merer, son of Sur/l, justified. (Simpson). Sur/l (swr), although not written syllabically, may well be a foreign name.

65 Simpson, BMMA 10.6 (1952), 185.

66 Helck, Beziehungen, 487, no. 15.

(for battle.)"[67]

(E30). Stele, U Penn E-13620. [Hitherto unpublished]. (Plate II). This is one of the Memphis stelae from the Clarence Fischer excavations, University Museum, University of Pennsylvania. It is of limestone, and measures 17 x 22.8 cm. It is badly chipped and cracked. The University Museum was at first hesitant to identify the deity as Rešep, but the iconography is unmistakable, and, if my reading is correct, ršp is clear in the inscription in the upper register.

In the upper register a man, woman and small boy approach Rešep, who stands facing to right. He is again wearing an Asiatic tasseled kilt almost identical to that on the Oriental Institute stele, E29, except that there are no crossed chest-bands. The crown is obliterated, but there are traces of tassels hanging down from the back. In his right hand Rešep holds a mace-axe below his waist, in his left a spear. Behind him is a "lute" symbol. In the lower register are a line of four worshippers, facing to left, before whom is an offering table. The iconography and style of the stele are those of the late Ramesside period.

(E31). Scarab Strassburg 1477.[68] Anepigraphic. Dated by Spiegelberg to the Nineteenth-Twentieth Dynasties. A figure, facing right, brandishes a mace-axe in his right hand, holds a spear and shield in his left. He wears an Upper Egyptian crown, and there is a quiver on his back.

(E32). Brussels Museum Fragment.[69] Unknown provenance. Wijngaarden published a photograph of this fragment, identifying the figure on it--broken off from the shoulders up--as Rešep. There is no legible inscription for verification, but the attribution seems certain. The figure strides to the right, a quiver on his back and a spear and shield in his left hand. His right arm is lifted over his head, but is broken off. The fringes at the bottom of the kilt are almost exactly the same as that of E29 and, indeed, the overall style of the two stelae is much the same.

(E33). Leibovitch Amulet.[70] Leibovitch obtained this tiny and very poorly executed votive object from a Cairo antiquities dealer, so its ultimate provenance is unknown. The figure on it, whom he probably correctly identifies as Rešep, carries in his right hand what may be a mace-axe. The right arm is flung clumsily to the side. In his left hand he holds a spear and a shield. His headgear is an Upper Egyptian crown. Before him is an altar, and beneath the whole scene are various cross-hatchings.

(E34). Stele Louvre 86.[71] We now proceed to a series of stelae,

67 Suggested to me by Prof. William Hallo of Yale.

68 Spiegelberg, OLZ 12 (1908), col. 530.

69 Wijngaarden, OMRO 10 (1932), 35 (Afb. 23).

70 Leibovitch, ASAE 39 (1939), 146-147.

71 Boreux, La stèle C. 86 du Musée du Louvre et les stèles similaires,"

all apparently of Theban (Deir el Medineh) provenance, on which Rešep is depicted together with Qudšu and Min. We will discuss this juxtaposition later. Two doubtful items not treated here are the gilded bronze amulet in the Athens Museum,[72] and the Stele Cairo = ANEP 470, which Müller interpreted as a Min-Qudšu-Rešep stele. His "Rešep" is evidently Seth.[73]

On the upper register[74] of the obverse of Louvre 86 are the three divinities, (ithyphallic) Min, Qudšu and Rešep, left to right, Min and Rešep facing in toward Qudšu who stands on a lion's back, facing front. Rešep wears the Upper Egyptian crown with two ribbons and a gazelle-head. He carries a lance in his right hand (resting its shaft on the floor) and an ʿankh in his left hand. He has a braided, typically Syrian beard. He is labeled ršpw nṯr ʿꜣ nb n nḥḥ ḥḳꜣ ḏt nb pḥty m ẖnw psḏt, "Rešep, the great god, lord of eternity, sovereign everlasting, mighty master, amidst the divine ennead."[75]

(E35). Vienna Stele.[76] Here are ithyphallic Min, Qudšu and Rešep disposed as on the previous stele. The figure of Rešep (here simply ršpw) is much abraded.

(E36). Stele Turin 1601.[77] Again, the three gods are posed as on E34, but Rešep carries a mace-axe at his side rather than an ʿankh. He is identified as ršpw nṯr ʿꜣ nb pt ḥḳꜣ nḫtw nṯr nḥḥ, "Rešep, great god, lord of the sky, master of power, everlasting god."[78]

(E37). Stele BM 560 [355].[79] A sepulchral stele of ḥrw, a judge.

---

in Mélanges syriens offerts à M. Rene Dussaud (Paris, 1939), II, 673-687, figs. 1, 2; Capart, ChrE 34 (1942), 239 [a review of Boreux]; de Rougé, "Lettre à Lejard," Oeuvres Diverse II [= Bib. Égyptologique 22] (Paris[?], 1852), 281-289, wherein Louvre 433 = Louvre C. 86; ANEP 474. (The work of Rougé is best found in libraries under F. Lejard, in Mémoires de l'académie des inscriptions et belles-lettres 20).

72 See W. Max Müller, Egyptological Researches: Results of a Journey in 1904 (Washington, D.C., 1906), 32 and Pl. 41b.

73 See ANEP 470 for remarks.

74 The lower register of the obverse and the entire reverse consist of votive and adorative statements pronounced by ḥwy and his family. The text contains many interesting epithets of Qudšu. (For a text and interpretation, see Stadelmann, Gottheiten, 121.)

75 Min is mnw ỉmn-rʿ ʿꜣ pḥty ḥry st·f wrt nṯr ʿꜣ and Qudšu is qdš nbt pt ẖnwt nṯrw nbw.

76 Boreux, in Mélanges Dussaud, 674, fig. 2.

77 Boreux, in Mélanges Dussaud, 681, fig. 3.

78 See K. H. Brugsch, Thesaurus Inscriptionum Aegypticarum: Altägyptische Inschriften (originally Leipzig, 1883-1891; reprinted Graz, 1968), V.VI., 1434; and R. Lanzone, Dizionario di mitologia egizia (Turin, 1881-1886), 1195-1197.

79 British Museum, Guidebook (1909), 180.

He and two members of his family offer homage to Qudšu (here knt),[80] Min and Rešep, who are posed as previously.

(E38). kꜣḥꜣ Stele, BM 646 [191].[81] Although Qudšu (knt) and Min are portrayed much as usual, the depiction of Rešep is unique. He stands holding a spear and an ʿankh. He wears a heavy beard and wig which is encircled by a fillet from which a gazelle-head projects in front. The way the fillet is attached, with cords down the back, is reminiscent of the Jewish tefillin. It is not impossible that the Egyptian uraeus, vulture and gazelle-head, and other Near Eastern frontlets have a common--if distant--apotropaic origin.

In the lower register are three figures making offerings to ʿAnat (ʿntt), who is seated on a throne. She holds a spear and shield in her right hand, a mace-axe in her left. Except for her long gown and the plumes of Maʿat on her crown, her iconography is identical to that of Rešep.[82] Significantly, Rešep and ʿAnat are often listed together in various Ugaritic ritual and sacrifice-list texts.

(E39). Stele Strassburg 1398.[83] Ramesside, from Simbillawein in the east Delta. This tiny anepigraphic stele has two registers. In the upper register are Horus and Ptah, with a third figure facing to the right which is surely Rešep: axe brandished over the head, shield in the left hand, quiver on his back, Upper Egyptian crown. Below are worshippers.

(E40). Stele of Matybaʿal, Aswan Museum 16.[84] Probably Ramesside, found in temple of Amenophis III at es-Seboua' in lower Nubia. In the upper register Amon-reʿ (ỉmn-rʿ nb n pꜣ mtnw, "Amon-reʿ, lord of the road") and Seth (stẖ ʿꜣ pḥty nb pt, "Seth, great in might, lord of the sky") sit enthroned. Below is Rešep facing right. Before him is an offering table and a worshipper. Rešep carries a mace-axe[85] in

80 On this "misspelling," see Helck, "Beiträge zu Syrien und Palästina in altägyptischer Zeit," AfO 22 (1968/69), 23; also Leibovitch, "Kent et Qadesh," Syria 38 (1961), 23-24.

81 British Museum, Guidebook (1909), 179-180 = ANEP 473. Also Stadelmann, Gottheiten, 119-120. For this and BM 650 [355], see also Boreux, in Mêlanges Dussaud, 675.

82 For ʿAnat thus, see H. Haussig in Götter und Mythen im Vorderen Orient [= Wörterbuch der Mythologie, I/1] (Stuttgart, 1965), Syria: 241 and Pl. III.

83 Spiegelberg, OLZ 12 (1908), col. 529 and Pl. 2; Leibovitch, ASAE 40 (1940), 172.

84 C. M. Firth, The Archaeological Survey of Nubia: Report for 1910-1911 (Cairo, 1927), 238-239; Leibovitch, ASAE 39 (1939), 155; Grdseloff, Les débuts, 5; Habachi, "Five Stelae from the Temple of Amenophis III at Es-Sebouaʿ now in the Aswan Museum," Kush 8 (1960), 50; Helck, Beziehungen, 497, no. 8.

85 So Habachi, who says that Firth's drawing, apparently indicating a spear, is inaccurate. (Kush 8, 50).

his relaxed right arm, a spear and shield in his left. He wears a Syrian tasseled garment and an Upper Egyptian crown with ribbons trailing behind. Rešep is simply ršpw. The worshipper is apparently Matyba'al.[86]

(E41). Abydos Stele, Mariette 1310.[87] Provenance and date uncertain, anepigraphic. A Rešep figure, standing right, brandishing a spear in his right hand, holding a spear and shield in his left. He wears an Upper Egyptian crown.

(E42). Müller Plaque.[88] There is a figure, probably Rešep, on this small anepigraphic plaque; he wears an Upper Egyptian crown with ribbons, brandishes a mace-axe in his right hand, holds a spear and shield in his left. He wears a conventionalized pointed beard.

(E43). Stele Zagazig, Cairo 71816.[89] Nineteenth or Twentieth Dynasty. This battered fragment of a crudely executed stele is anepigraphic, and shows the remains of a standing figure, facing left, probably Rešep. His left arm is damaged, but clearly brandishes a weapon over his head. In his right hand is a shield. He wears a beribboned Upper Egyptian crown, apparently with a uraeus in front.

(E44). Texts of the Mortuary Temple of Ramses III.[90] Twentieth Dynasty, Medinet Habu. In the "Inscription of the Year Five" of the Medinet Habu series of texts commemorating the Lybian victories of Ramses III, Rešep is again associated with horsemanship. Interestingly, Montu (see E5) occurs in the immediate context: "The chariot-warriors are as mighty as Rešeps [sic].[91] They look upon myriads as

86 The worshipper is a foreigner, as indicated by the boomerang-determinative following his name. Grdseloff, Les débuts, 5, reads his name as ḳmꜣ-bʿl, " Baʿal a crée," but Habachi's reading, Kush 8 (1960), 50, is preferable: mꜣʿtybʿl = Matybaʿal, "Righteous is Baʿal." "Righteous of Baʿal" seems to me equally plausible. For an analysis of this and similar names, see Habachi, 50, n. 18.

87 A.Mariette, Catalogue général des monuments d'Abydos découverts pendant les fouilles de cette ville (Paris, 1875), 497, no. 1310; also Spiegelberg, "Neue Rescheph-Darstellungen," OLZ 12 (1908), cols. 529-532 with Plates; Stadelmann, Gottheiten, 72.

88 W. Max Müller, Egyptological Researches: Results of a Journey in 1904 (Washington, D.C., 1906), 33.

89 Leibovitch, ASAE 39 (1939), 154; Helck, Beziehungen, 486, no. 6.

90 W. F. Edgerton and J. A. Wilson, Historical Records of Ramses III: The Texts in Medinet Habu [= SAOC 12] (Chicago, 1936), 23-24.

91 Commentators (in addition to Edgerton and Wilson, see Grdseloff, Les débuts, 19; and Simpson, Or 29, 65) call attention to the plural: Rešeps. In context it does not seem to me unusual--each man was like a Rešep," they were so many Rešeps"--much like the California idiom referring to tanned younged surfers as "sun-bronzed Apollos." "Rešeps" does not imply a plurality within the god any more than "Apollos" does. For this reason it is difficult to agree with Grdseloff: "Au moins jusqu'au Ve siècle avant J.-Ch., ce dieu y fut adoré à côte d'ʿAnat comme principale

mere drops. (Ramses') strength is before them like Montu; his name and the terror of him burn up the plains and the hill countries."

(E45). Papyrus Wilbour, Vs B8, 22.[92] Ramses V. Under the general heading of "Khato-land of Pharaoh under his authority starting from the backland of Heracleopolis in Memphis (on) the East Bank (administered) by the hand of the deputy Ḥori," there is a theophoric toponym: [tꜣ] ỉnt ršpw, "the Valley of Rešep."[93]

(E46). Ostracon Cairo 25063.[94] Ramses VI, Biban el Molouk, tomb no. 9). The black and red figure on this ostracon is doubtlessly Rešep. His right arm, broken off the fragment, was evidently over his head holding a weapon. His left hand holds a spear and a quite elaborate shield. There is a quiver from his right shoulder, and his Upper Egyptian crown has a gazelle-head in front.[95]

(E47). Drexel Statuette.[96] Late Dynastic period. A figure,

---

divinité, sous divers noms, tel que ršp ḥṣ, 'Rechef à la flèche,' ou ršp mkl, 'Rechef-Moukal.' Cette pluralité des Rechef était d'ailleurs un fait connu des Égyptiens [dans le texte de Medinet Habu]."

92 A. H. Gardiner, Ed., The Wilbour Papyrus, III: Translation (Oxford, 1948), 114.

93 As Gardiner indicates in his commentary (Wilbour II, 176-178, 191), the topographical problems connected with the names in Section B of this text border on the hopeless. Simpson, Or 29, 67-68, following the general geography proposed by Gardiner, would place the "Valley of Rešep" "just north of the Herakleopolitan nome on the east bank." He sees this as appropriate, since "Rešep is always connected with the east in Egyptian groupings of gods." He is here evidently referring to his remarks on this phenomenon as evidence on the Turin Altar (E50) which he discusses in the same article. I am aware of no other "Egyptian grouping of gods" which would be relevant here. The phenomenon of Rešep's association with Herakleopolis, however, might find greater support. See Simpson, 69, and E49.

That a valley should bear Rešep's name attests to the considerable status he enjoyed in the late Ramesside period. Simpson sees this as Rešep having found a "home" or principal cult place in Herakleopolis during his "Egyptian career." Says Helck, Beziehungen, 488, "Sogar ein Tal südlich Memphis auf dem Ostufer in der 20, Dynastie als 'Tal des Reschef' bezeichnet, wohl weil man den Gott dort wohnen glaubte."

94 Published in M. G. Daressy, Catalogue général des antiquités du Musée du Caire, Nos. 25001-25385 (Cairo, 1900), 13, no. 25063 and Pl. XIII; also Helck, Beziehungen, 487 and Müller, Researches, 33 and Pl. 41/2.

95 The inscription, which is not clear on either Daressy's or Müller's photograph, is fragmentary: [ ]m st-šwꜣ[ ]y ỉt·f sḏm-ʿš st-šw-kꜣ-sꜣ.

96 Sỉmpson, "An Egyptian Statuette of a Phoenician God," BMMA 10:6, 183-187. Acquired by the Metropolitan Museum in 1889 from Joseph Drexel, this statue was first noticed by Max Müller in 1906 in his Researches, 33, n. 2. Although there are many so-called "Rešep-bronzes" extant, this is the only known stone sculpture of Rešep in the round.

surely Rešep, with raised weapon, shield, and a gazelle-head on his crown.[97]

(E48). Relief, Temple of Mut in Karnak.[98] Time of Taharqa, Twenty-fifth Dynasty. On the wall of the room of Montu-em-hat is a relief on which many cult-objects are portrayed, one of which, possibly a pectoral, has a probable image of Rešep.[99]

(E49). Relief, North Wall of Sanctuary A, Temple of Hibis, El Khargeh Oasis.[100] Twenty-seventh Dynasty. The Temple of Hibis was apparently commissioned by Darius II.[101] In the third register of this relief, in a procession of some thirty deities and other figures, is Rešep. Davies reads "Rešep, son of the lord of Anhas."[102] Simpson,[103] perhaps because of the generally scrambled order of the hieroglyphs, suggests "the son of Rešep, the lord of Heracleopolis," as a possible alternative.[104] In this scene Rešep wears the high Upper

97 The statuette is broken at the front base with the left foot missing. The back pilaster, peculiarly shaped to support Rešep's weapon, is broken at the top right, but (from a personal inspection of the statuette) the weapon appears to be a mace-axe, not a club. The general handling of the musculature and the relative proportions are rather poor, but he is obviously meant to be portrayed as a vigorous warrior. He wears a short battle kilt. The crown with the fronting gazelle-head is rather flat, possibly to avoid breaking. It may be for a similar reason that Rešep's usual spear is omitted and that the shield is reduced to a minimum, blended with the kilt for support. The statuette is anepigraphic, although there may have been an inscription on the front part of the pedestal which is broken off.

98 Wijngaarden, OMRO 10 (1932), 34; Simpson, Or 29 (1960), 68. From Mariette, Karnak (Paris, 1875), 64-65 and Pl. 43.

99 Simpson's description: "[There are] figures of three gods, none of whom is supplied with an identifying label. One of them holds a shield in his left hand and a spear with a curved end in his right hand. He wears the white crown decorated with a fillet. In view of these iconographic features there is a possibility that the god Rešep is represented, although one feature, the gazelle, is lacking." The central figure is surely Qudšu. She stands on a lion's back, holding a serpent and lotuses, much like Qudšu on E34. Wijngaarden also notes here Qudšu-like attributes.

100 N. de Garies Davies, The Temple of Hibis in El Khārgeh Oasis, Part III: The Decoration [The Metropolitan Museum of Art Egyptian Expedition, XVII] (New York, 1953), 6 and Pl. 3. Also Leclant, Syria 37 (1960), 49ff.

101 See Gardiner, Egypt of the Pharaohs, 542.

102 Ahnas = nnỉ-nsw = Herakleopolis. See Davies, 6. On the possibility that Rešep may have been confused with Ḥry-šf, see Leclant, Syria 37 (1960), 53; Simpson, Or 29 (1960), 68, and Chapter IID of this study.

103 Simpson, Or 29 (1960), 69.

104 The prior translation seems to me more probable, but Simpson points out that many of the gods represented in the total relief are asso-

Egyptian crown. He carries a knife in either hand shaped like the hieroglyphic reed-leaf. He is preceded by three ʿAstarte figures.[105]

(E50). Turin Altar.[106] Nectanebo II, Thirtieth Dynasty. Unknown provenance. Toward the end of the native Egyptian dynasties, there is an occurence of the name of Rešep on the so-called Turin Altar, amongst a list of gods of which sixty-eight are legible. Rešep is listed alongside ʿAnat[107] among the deities of the eastern quadrant of the sky, and the reference is apparently to a chapel: ršp m ḥwt ršp, "Rešep in the chapel of Rešep," although some would take m-ḥwt-ršp as a toponym.[108] Either interpretation would seem to indicate the existence of a cult-place of the god.

(E51). Mural, Temple of Montu at Karnak.[109] Ptolemy III Euergetes (246-221 B.C.). The inscription on this mural is ḏd-mdw mnw smꜣ ḫftyw [ ] ršp ḥr-ib pr mntw, etc., "Pronouncement of Min who slaughters enemies [ ] Rešep who dwells in the abode of Montu, etc." The iconography of Rešep is unusual.[110] The inscription which links Rešep both with Min (albeit indirectly) and Montu seems to imply that Rešep, by dwelling in Montu's abode, has somehow replaced the function and position of Montu in the Ptolemaic Egyptian pantheon.

---

ciated with Herakleopolis.

105 Simpson mentions and seems to have noticed two, perhaps because of the cropping of the photograph he received from William Hayes, and which he publishes in his article, Pl. 2. ʿAstarte's name is misspelled as ʿsṯt, i.e., without the -r-, but it is hard to believe any other goddess is intended.

106 Simpson, Or 29 (1960), 69. The altar is illustrated in Habachi, "A Statue of Bakenniffi, Nomarch of Athribis during the Invasion of Egypt by Assurbanipal," MDIK 15 (1957), Pl. 8,9.

107 For a discussion of this juxtaposition see T. Gaster, "Groupings of Deities in the Ritual Tariffs from Ras Shamra-Ugarit," AfO 12 (1938/39), 148. Among Gaster's remarks: "It is interesting to observe in this connection that Drexler (in Roscher's Lex. Myth. II, p. 1117) identifies the Keraúnios and Keraúnia of the Cypriot tomb inscription, Waddington III, 2739, with ršp ḥṣ and ʿnt.

108 W. Golenischeff, "Über zwei Darstellungen des Gottes Antaeus," ZÄS 20 (1882), 142, note 2; W. Budge, The Gods of the Egyptians (Dover ppbk. reprint: New York, 1969), II, pp. 282-283.

109 Leibovitch, ASAE 39 (1939), 157-158, Pl. XX. Originally published in Lepsius, Denkmäler, IV, Pl. II.

110 Ptolemy is depicted on the right with a subdued enemy, as if presenting him to the god standing before him. One would have expected this god to be Min, and some have so described him (e.g., Leibovitch, ASAE 39 [1939], 158), but he does not at all fit Min's iconography. It seems to be more like Rešep's in several ways. The god holds a ceremonial mace in his right hand and a staff or spear in his left. He wears the Upper Egyptian crown (with no emblem in front nor ribbons, however), and his tight kilt is typical of other Rešep representations.

(E52). The MKL Stele of Beisan.[111]

(E53). Lachish Prism.[112] Albright dates to c. 1435 B.C., suspects that the image on the fourth face of the prism is Rešep.

(E54). The so-called Rešep Bronzes. Not much will be said here about the so-called Rešep bronzes and related statuettes which have been found all over the Mediterranean Near East--Egypt (especially the Delta area), Palestine, Phoenicia, Syria, Anatolia, Cyprus, Greece--except to voice a strong word of caution. They date mostly to the middle of the Second Millenium, B.C.

They have been variously classified,[113] and obviously there is a good deal of guesswork in tagging these bronzes with gods' names. Unfortunately, none of these statues has an inscription, and the finds have been sufficiently random so that they cannot be connected with particular gods by archaeological association. There is no question that many of these bronzes could be Rešep, but in view of the number of gods in the Levant (the Egyptian bronzes seem to be of Syrian manufacture or inspiration) who have the martial characteristics exemplified on these statuettes, it is hazardous to use the evidence of the bronzes to establish anything definite about the nature of Rešep, tempting as it is.

Suffice it to say that if a large number of these widely-found statuettes were indeed Rešep, it would certainly attest to the wide-spread knowledge and cult of the god.[114]

111 Because of its special nature, this stele will be treated below (Chapter IIC) with the Cypriot epigraphic material.

112 Albright, The Proto-Sinaitic Inscriptions and Their Decipherment [= Harvard Theological Studies XXII] (Cambridge, second ed., 1969), 5 and figs. 2,3.

113 Stadelmann, Gottheiten, 49-52, speaks of the "Rešep-type" (the left foot is forward, his right arm is uplifted--evidently with a weapon --and his left hand is held out front; he usually has a high Upper Egyptian crown), a "Baʿal-Hadad-type" (much like the "Rešep-type;" the crown generally has horns), and the "Tešub-type" (similar, but with Hittite headgear and clothing). See alternate classifications in Vattioni, AION 15 (1965), 30ff. For the most pertinent examples, see Du Mesnil du Buisson, Études sur les dieux phéniciens hérités par l'Empire Romain (Leiden, 1970), xvi, fig. 40, which is a suggested reconstruction of Dussaud, L'Art phénicien du IIe Millénaire (Paris, 1949), 68, fig. 34 (orig. pub. in Syria 10 [1932], Pl. LIII, by Schaeffer, = ANEP 481); also ANEP 496; Dussaud, L'Art, 66, fig. 29; Roeder (see next note), 37; Dussaud, L'Art, 76, fig 45.

114 One of the most thorough treatments of these bronzes is G. Roeder, Ägyptische Bronzefiguren [= Mitteilungen aus der Ägyptischen Sammlung (Berlin Museum), VI] (Berlin, 1956, in which he discusses not only those of Egyptian provenance, but many others as well.

C. GODS ASSOCIATED WITH REŠEP

Qudšu (E34-38) is surely to be identified with the Canaanite-Hebrew Ašerah (Ugaritic *aṯrt*). Qudšu, "holy"--in this context with some of the same connotations that attach to the Hebrew *qadeš*, "a sacred person" = "a temple prostitute"--is admittedly an epithet which could be applied to more than one goddess. ʿAstarte and ʿAnat, however, have distinctive iconographies and onomastica in Egypt, in each case different from those associated with Qudšu.[115] Note that Qudšu and ʿAnat are contrasted on the *ḳꜣḥꜣ* stele.[116]

115 For arguments largely contrary to what I propose here, see Stadelmann, *Gottheiten*, 113ff. Note, incidentally, that R. Du Mesnil du Buisson, *Études*,134, labels the figure of an explicit Qudšu stele simply as ʿAstarte. See also remarks of Gaster, *JQR* 37 (1947), 289 (8).

116 There is little to support the hypothesis of LeLasseur, *Les déesses armées dans l'art classique grec et leur origines orientales* (Paris, 1919), 229, that Qudšu is the erotic and ʿAnat the martial manifestation of ʿAstarte/Ištar, nor the scheme of Stadelmann, *Gottheiten*, 115, whereby Qudšu is the "holiness" alternately of ʿAnat and ʿAstarte.

Ašerah in Ugaritic literature is the "Lady of the Sea," the "Progenitress of the Gods." Once (*UT* 51, iii) she is the hostess at a banquet which Baʿal finds lewd and shameful. In the *OT* worship of Ašerah is a perennial threat to the Hebrew faith. [See esp. *2 Kgs* 23:4-7.] One gathers that wooden plaques and other images of her were common [*1 Kgs* 13:13, *2 Kgs* 21:7 *et alibi*], and at Mount Carmel there were "four hundred prophets of Ašerah" [*1 Kgs* 18:10].

It seems quite possible that the goddess Ašerah of the *OT* corresponds to the unnamed goddess (often in the identical pose and with the same Hathor-wig as the Egyptian Qudšu), whose plaques and figurines abound in Palestine from c. 2000, B.C., onwards. (See *ANEP* 469, esp. the first two figs. Helck, *Beziehungen*, 497-499, provides a list of various Egyptian stelae of Qudšu). It is these figurines and plaques which might provide the necessary link between the erotic *OT*/Ugaritic goddess whose images are frequently alluded to in the *OT*, and the Egyptian Qudšu, "Queen of the Sky," "Queen of the Gods," "Offspring of Reʿ," whose iconography is almost identical with that of the goddess of the figurines. (See remarks of Stadelmann, *Gottheiten*, 111.)

T. Yamashita (*The Goddess Asherah*, Yale University dissertation, 1963, unpublished) argues strongly that Qudšu and Ašerah are not to be identified. His argumentation, however, is based almost exclusively on the interpretation of four Ugaritic texts, and does not give enough weight to other evidence. Two dissertations, one on ʿAnat, another on ʿAstarte, are currently in preparation at the University of California and the Graduate Theological Union, Berkeley, which hopefully will resolve some of the vexing problems of the Northwest Semitic goddesses in general.

To place Min, the god of fertility, alongside Qudšu is prima facie understandable. But what is Rešep doing with them? Is there a common theme, and if so, is that theme fertility?

Both Albright[117] and Dahood[118] stress the "polar" or contradictory aspect of some gods' characteristics, including Rešep. If there is a god of light, for example, he is likely to be also the god of darkness, etc. Thus, according to Albright, we should not be surprised to find this tendency manifested in a composite deity, Rešep-Šulman (E13). One would expect Rešep, the argument goes, as the god of disease or death, also to be the god of healing, fruitfulness, etc. Perhaps he is to be thought of as a chthonic deity, involved with the natural forces of life and death. On this score, as Šulman was a god of well-being (and as such, identifiable with Apollo's aspect of healer and benefactor), and as Rešep was a god of ill-being (and as such identifiable with Apollo's bow-and-arrow pestilential aspect), it was natural for the two to merge.[119]

If this polarization was true, are we to think of Rešep on the Min-Qudšu-Rešep stelae as paradoxically representing fertility, life and well-being, as opposed to his better attested negative role? There can be no question that Rešep is portrayed in a benevolent role on these stelae, as well as on a few other stelae of possibly Asiatic (in Egypt) origin.[120] Strongly supporting this is the fact that, contrary to almost every other known portrayal of Rešep, on this series of stelae he does not assume a warlike stance. His weapon is resting at his side, while his other hand holds an ʿankh, the symbol of life. One is reminded of the Karatepe inscription where Rešep is spoken of as a god of well-being

117 Albright, Archaeology and the Religion of Palestine, (Fifth ed., Baltimore, 1968), 77-78.

118 In S. Moscati, Ed., Le antiche divinità semitiche (Rome, 1958), 84.

119 See also M. Astour, Hellenosemitica (Leiden, 1967), 310ff. Dahood (in Divinità, 65) says "This apparent contradiction finds its sharpest expression in the composite deity Rašap-Šalmon. . . . This composite deity illustrates the strong and constant tendency of Canaanite and Phoenician religious belief and practice to bring opposites together. Polarities were felt to be of the very essence of life."

120 E.g., E19. It is likely that several of the even warlike Rešep stelae from Deir el Medineh are the products of Syrian workmen.

and abundance.

But the question remains: is this portrayal of Rešep in a benevolent role on these stelae purely a result of some inherent polarity, or are there other factors at work? Let us turn momentarily to the Rešep-Šulman stele, cited by Albright as an obvious example of the polarity of Rešep's attributes--a view that presupposes the basically positive nature of Šulman.

Albright, who wrote in 1942[121] that "Rešep was somehow connected with pestilence, whereas Shulmân-Eshmûn was a god of healing," had written ten years earlier[122] that "Šulmânu [as] a god of welfare is a euphemism," since he is a god of the underworld. Albright admitted to a certain paradox, however: "gods of healing are necessarily connected with the underworld." Albright considered Šulman a natively Mesopotamian god identified with Ešmun, later adopted by the Canaanites.[123]

Šulman can perhaps be identified with the Ugaritic god šlm, god of sunset, in the pair šḥr/šlm.[124] In a central Arabian Liḥyanite inscription of the last third of the first millenium, B.C.,[125] he is apparently a god of death and the underworld, and is either linked to or identified with Abû-Îlâf, a god who has the same role. Two or three centuries later he occurs in a Palmyrene inscription[126] where he is paired with Abgal, the horse-riding god. Dussaud[127] cites

121 Albright, Archaeology and the Religion of Palestine, 79.

122 "The Syro-Mesopotamian God Shulmân-Eshmûn and Related Figures," AfO 7 (1931/32), 168.

123 In these views Albright is followed by several authors. See, e.g., Dahood in Divinità, 85, and Stadelmann, Gottheiten, 61ff.

124 For more information on this pair, see Pope in Haussig, Götter und Mythen, 306; Roberts, The Earliest Semitic Pantheon, 51; and Gaster, Thespis (Rev., New York, 1961), 411. For Šulman/Šalim, see Lewy, JBL 59 (1940), 519ff.

125 W. Caskel, Lihyan und Lihyanisch (Köln, 1954), 116-117, no. 82. For the link with Abû-Îlâf, see also nos. 72, 77. For Šalmân in north and central Arabia, see M. Höfner in Haussig, Götter und Mythen, 466.

126 D. Schlumberger, La Palmyrène du Nord-ouest [= Bib. Arch. et Hist. XLIX] (Paris, 1951), 136, no. 38. He discusses here also the otherwise unknown god ʾr/dgy, also associated with Šalmân.

127 R. Dussaud, La pénétration des Arabes en Syrie avant l'Islam [= Bib. Arch. et Hist. LIX] (Paris, 1955), 132.

the Palmyrene inscription as an instance of Syrian influence on the Arabs as they penetrated north and settled; Šulman (Palmyrene, probably Šalmân) was taken over with the associations the Syrians had already attached to him.

The evidence would suggest that contrary to Albright's view that Šulman was an Assyrian god adopted by the Canaanites, he seems rather to have been a West Semitic god adopted into the Assyrian pantheon which, in Albright's own words,[128] "was incredibly composite, with gods of every possible origin, who were identified with each other, quite regardless of ultimate origin and primary nature." It is at least possible that Šulman was quite secondary in the Canaanite pantheon, too, and was originally not a god of the more sophisticated city-folk, but an Arabian desert god, gradually assimilated west and northeast into the more urban regions.

Despite the several occurences of Šulman in Mesopotamian onomastica,[129] Albright's arguments for his importance in the Assyrian pantheon are not convincing. His thesis that Šulman is to be identified with Ešmun is probably also to be discarded.[130]

Whatever his origin, Šulman's name is somewhat misleading. The god seems to partake of the "shadier" connotations of the root ŠLM: "coming to an end, death, corpse, sundown, etc."[131] It is not so much that Šulman is euphemistically or ironically named, it is apparently that the root itself is patient of these negative meanings. Although the particular noun-form Šulman might argue against it, it is even quite possible that various D-stem meanings underlie the name: "requite, revenge, etc."[132]

128 AfO 7 (1931/2), 164.

129 See C. Saporetti, Onomastica Medio-Assira [= Studia Pohl 6] (Rome, 1970), I, 467-470 and II, 162, 172.

130 See Dussaud, La pénétration des Arabes, 132 and n. 3.

131 See instances cited by Albright, AfO 7 (1931/32), 168; also references in Schlumberger, La Palmyrène, 136.

132 We may, I believe, safely ignore opinions which see other than ŠLM underlying Šulman, e.g., M. Lidzbarski, ZfA 20 (1898), 328: "Der Gott Ršp findet sich häufig in cyprisch-phönizischen Inschriften, und zwar mit einem Stadtnamen dahinter. Daher kann Š/Slmn das cyprische Salamís, und Ršp-Š/Slmn ein Apóllôn Salamínios sein."

From the above it can be seen that the juxtaposition of Rešep and Šulman may not be so paradoxical after all. Significantly, it is the usual martial iconography of Rešep that prevails on the Aberdeen ršp-šꜣrmꜥnꜣ stele. This stele dates to the "Syrophile" period of the Eighteenth Dynasty following Thutmosis III, when contact with the Syrian desert through war made Syrian gods popular in Egypt.[133]

Let us return to the Min-Qudšu-Rešep stelae. Stadelmann, Boreux and Capart (following Boreux)[134] all propose, with varying qualifications, that these stelae, mostly attributable to Deir el Medineh in the Nineteenth Dynasty, are the products of Syrian workmen imported into Thebes under the Ramesside pharaohs to exercise their various crafts, and that they all bear the earmarks of a particularized local cult.[135]

It is important to note that until late times Rešep appears in nothing but an aggressive warlike role on reliefs and stelae of demonstrably through-and-through Egyptian manufacture. It is only on those of apparently Syrian workmanship in Egypt or those easily susceptible of such attribution that he takes on a more positive character. It is possible that his warlike and pestilential tendencies at home in Syria (and as borrowed by the Egyptians) became a source of protection when abroad. His martial qualities for the expatriate Syrians would not be something to fear, but a security umbrella. As such he would have been raised to the level of a special patron and given a more cosmic status, and so share in the level of Qudšu's exalted epithets. On these stelae he is "lord of the sky," "mighty amidst the ennead."

If this hypothesis is true, Qudšu would be the main object of the stelae, since she was the special female patron of the expatriate Syrians. Min and Rešep were chosen as coconsorts, Min because he was a popular god in Thebes and

133 See remarks in Stadelmann, Gottheiten, 56.

134 Stadelmann, Gottheiten, 118. Stadelman says elsewhere, however, perhaps implying that in his view the workmen were not necessarily Asiatic, that Qudšu, Min and Rešep could have been thought of as chthonic deities appropriate for a necropolis (138ff.); Boreux, in Mélanges Dussaud, 679ff., Capart, ChrE 34 (1942), 239.

135 See Boreux, in Mélanges Dussaud, 679ff.

made a natural mate for Qudšu, and Rešep because he, too, was a special patron, and not because he shared the same fertility theme common to Min and Qudšu.

I am reminded of the situation in certain Christian communities where Mary and other saints develop a role of such cosmic proportions that their cult often threatens orthodox Christian tradition. The case of Michael the archangel in some Latin countries is particularly parallel.

D. REŠEP'S WEAPONS

In addition to the spear which Rešep generally carries in the same hand with his shield, Rešep usually brandishes another weapon over his head.[135a] In the extant Egyptian representations of him, the weapon is once (E29) a fenestrated axe (Yadin[136] calls it an "eye-axe"), occasionally a plain mace of the "apple" variety,[137] a spear, or knives (E49).

More characteristic of Rešep, however, is the mace-axe, an instrument composed of a metal blade with a stone affixed to its juncture with the shaft to give the weapon greater striking weight. This weapon is also associated with ʿAnat in Egyptian iconography.

As Leibovitch[138] has pointed out, this weapon seems to be of Asiatic origin. It possibly may have been in actual combat use in Asia, although in Egypt it apparently was a primarily ceremonial symbol of Asiatic gods, specifically of war gods.[139]

135a For a general, but dated, discussion of Rešep's weapons, see Golenischeff, ZÄS 20 (1882), 141.

136 Y. Yadin, The Art of Warfare in Biblical Lands in the Light of Archaeological Study (New York, 1963), I, 12 and passim in the first 12 pp.

137 See Yadin, Art of Warfare, I, 11.

138 Leibovitch, ASAE 39 (1939), 153-154.

139 See Leibovitch, as above, fig. 8, examples of this weapon as depicted on reliefs of various tombs, etc., beginning with the Eighteenth Dynasty. Note in this figure that the ʿḥꜣ-sign, written in the Old Kingdom generally with a mace, and in the Middle Kingdom generally with an axe, is often, from the Eighteenth Dynasty onwards, written with a mace-axe. Yadin, Art of Warfare, I, 194, publishes a line-drawing of a row of Asiatic tribute-bearers from a wall-painting (Tomb of Iamanezeh) of the time

In several instances it is difficult to determine if the weapon that Rešep brandishes is a mace-axe or simply a mace of the "apple" variety with a twist in the middle. It is also possible that in some depictions of Rešep which we know only from pre-Twentieth Century line-drawings, what was drawn as a spear may actually have been a thin mace-axe.

E. REŠEP AND THE GAZELLE

One of the features most persistently associated with Rešep in Egyptian iconography is the gazelle or the gazelle-head. In approximately a dozen of the fifty-odd items I have cataloged,[140] Rešep appears with a gazelle-head on the front of his Upper Egyptian crown, once (E38) on a fillet. There is also the probability that on the Gebel Agg graffito (E8) the gifts of a bow, arrows and a gazelle are intended for Rešep.

Although I am convinced the symbol of the gazelle must have desert or martial connotations and has nothing to do with fertility as some have suggested, unfortunately I have nothing new to offer to shed light on this vexing problem.[141] The question of horns rather than a gazelle-head has been mentioned in connection with E14.[142]

---

of Thutmosis III-Amenophis II. What one of these bearers is carrying is surely a mace-axe, although Yadin describes it only as a mace. Another example is on the pectoral of Ammenemes III, Twelfth Dynasty, from Dahshur: Yoyotte, Treasures of the Pharaohs (Geneva, 1968), 55. The pectoral could well be of a much later date, despite the cartouche of Ammenemes.

140 E10, E19, E27, E28, E29, E35, E36, E37, E46, E47, E49.

141 For discussion, see esp. Simpson, BMMA 10:6 (1952), 186; an early article of Albright, "Gilgames and Engidu," JAOS 40 (1920), 328ff.; and the many references passim in Gese, Höfner and Rudolph, Die Religionen Altsyriens, Altarabiens und der Mandäer [= Die Religionen der Menschheit, 10/2] (Stuttgart, 1970). Also H. Thompson, MEKAL: The God of Beth-Shan (Leiden, 1970), 152-157.

142 Horns have been associated with Šedu, Mikal, Seth and possibly other deities. There is no instance where horns can clearly be associated with Rešep. Grdseloff, Les débuts, Pl. IIIb = Leibovitch, ASAE 48 (1948), figs. 81, 82, identifies the horned god(s) of a Cypriot cylinder seal with Rešep, but Leibovitch, ASAE 42 (1942), 437ff., has convincingly rejected this view. Virolleaud, Ugaritica V (Paris, 1968), 550, has suggested that ḥby bʿl qrnm in RS 24.258, "the demon (creeper?) of the baʿal (possessor?)

F. REŠEP IN EGYPT: BRIEF RÉSUMÉ

Stadelmann[143] and others have written at length about the role of Rešep in Egypt, a topic which is best viewed in the context of Rešep in the Near East in general, but it will be of purpose here to make at least a few summary observations.

The dating of at least a dozen major items pertaining to Rešep is doubtful, especially of those vaguely attributed to the Eighteenth or Nineteenth Dynasties. Hopefully a more accurate chronology may sometime be established for this crucial period.

Until the end of the Middle Kingdom Rešep's presence in Egypt is attested only in a foreign personal name. With the advent of the New Kingdom, however, contact between Egypt and the Asiatic cultures to the northeast became greatly intensified.[144] There is evidence that Egypt enjoyed a certain Syrophile fad under and immediately after Thutmosis III. Stadelmann[145] also notes that there may have been work centers in Egypt where Asiatic influence was especially strong. Amenophis II lived in one such area, prw-nfr, as a youth. It seems that it was under this pharaoh, the last of the kings of this period to wage extensive campaigns into Syria, that the cult of Rešep and certain other Asiatic gods was introduced formally into Egypt, with Rešep precisely as a royal patron. There is no evidence as yet that his influence went beyond the pharaoh to the people in a popular

---

of the two horns," refers to Rešep. In context this is hardly likely. El is reeling with hallucinations in a drunken stupor, and the situation demands some subjectively conjured-up chimera. There are no good grounds for labeling this monster Rešep.

The gazelle-head is also found on the crown of Ḳeserti and Šedu. (See Leibovitch, ASAE 48 [1948], 435-444; also Helck, Beziehungen, 499). Certainly Šedu and probably Ḳeserti manifest warlike characteristics similar to those of Rešep; likely the gazelle-head here has the same symbolic force as with Rešep. See now also Thompson, MEKAL (Leiden, 1970), 144ff.

143 To date Stadelmann has made the most thorough attempt to analyse the role of Rešep in Egypt, Gottheiten, 21ff., 56ff., 134ff.

144 See Helck in Haussig, Götter und Mythen, 317.

145 Stadelmann, Gottheiten, 56.

146 Grdseloff, Les débuts, 1-7.

cult at this time.[147]

Rešep, as Amenophis II's special military patron, was the divine embodiment of Amenophis' prowess, and seemed to have the functions that Montu hitherto enjoyed. He is, indeed, frequently mentioned in connection (or in identification?) with Montu.

Exactly why Amenophis II chose Rešep, a god of an alien people, as one of his personal patrons remains a mystery. Most hypotheses put forward are not persuasive. Grdseloff[148] proposes that the Syrian Rešep was particularly suited to the spirit and mystique of the Egyptians as their religious and cultural horizons broadened at the beginning of the Eighteenth Dynasty. Meyer[149] suggests that the Egyptians stood in wonder at the might of the Syrian gods--an hypothesis difficult to understand in light of the historical circumstances. Stadelmann[150] suggests largely political reasons, but also influence from Egyptian soldiers and administrators stationed in Asia. He maintains, probably correctly, that the first manifestations of these Asiatic gods in Egypt were in a military context.

On the other hand, it may have been that Amenophis II was a rugged individualist like his successor Amenophis IV, and experienced a certain personal fascination for the Asiatic gods then becoming known in Egypt, and fancied Rešep as a fine god who captured his own military spirit in a peculiar way.

After Amenophis II, occurrences of Rešep gradually trickle off with his less militarily inclined successors of the Eighteenth Dynasty, until the Ramesside times, when Rešep enjoys a remarkable popular resurgence. At this period Rešep seems no longer to be a personal patron of the pharaoh, but a god of the common people. Yet there seems to remain some continuity in his cult from the Eighteenth Dynasty, man-

147 Note the distinction made in Stadelmann, Gottheiten, 134ff., between "Königsgottheiten" and "Volksgottheiten."

148 Grdseloff, Les débuts, 1-7, and as cited by Stadelmann, Gottheiten 21.

149 Meyer, ZDMG 31 (1878), 725ff., and as cited by Stadelmann, Gottheiten, 22. Stadelmann calls Meyer's views "reichlich unägyptisch."

150 Stadelmann, Gottheiten, 20ff. and 135ff.

ifested in basically the same iconography (but becoming more standardized) and in the retention of certain thematic associations. Many of the people from whom the Ramesside stelae emanate seem to have been Syrians working in Egypt. With them, and possibly with the common folk of Egypt with whom they lived, Rešep was still a war god, but apparently conceived of in benign, positive terms, often linked with the Syrian Qudšu and the popular Egyptian Min.

After the Nineteenth Dynasty, as the second millenium drew to a close, Rešep's cult in Egypt is still sporadically attested into Ptolemaic times, during which period it became progressively more affected by the religious syncretism and general breakdown in traditional national pantheons that followed upon the traumatic hellenization of the eastern Mediterranean area.

Chapter II: Semitic Evidence

A. ONOMASTICA

To date the most thorough treatment of Rešep in Semitic sources is F. Vattioni's "Il dio Resheph," AION 15 (1965), 39-74.[151] It would be pointless to repeat his research here, but in several instances it is necessary to update it and occasionally to make minor corrections. D. Conrad[152] has also written a monograph on Rešep which is often provocative on points of mythological interpretation,[153] but highly eclectic both in methodology and in the use of evidence.

Rešep appears in a rich variety of proper names in Semitic sources. The oldest set of attestations is from Mari,[154] where the Akkadian I-din-^{d}ru-úš-pa-an (occuring also at Terqa as I-din-ru-uš-pa-an, and at Ḫana),[155] Ia-aḫ-zu-[ub/ur?]-^{d}ra-ša-ap,[156] and the apparently Amorite A-bi-ra-sa-ap occur. In Sargonid times the name I-zi-ra-sa-ap occurs.[157] Izi in this Amorite name is problematic.[158]

151 = Annali, Istituto Universitario Orientale di Napoli, Nuova Serie.

152 D. Conrad, "Der Gott Reschef," ZAW 83 (1971), 157-183.

153 Which is to say, I strongly disagree with most of what he proposes.

154 See J. Lewy, "Naḫ et Rušpān," in Mélanges Dussaud, I, 275; Vattioni, AION 15 (1965), 42; Gelb, Glossary of Old Akkadian [= Materials for the Chicago Assyrian Dictionary, 3] (Chicago, 1957), 236; H. Huffmon, Amorite Personal Names in the Mari Texts (Baltimore, 1956), 263, 185, 192.

155 Lewy, Mélanges Dussaud, 273; Huffmon, Amorite Personal Names, 263. For Ḫana, see Vattioni, 42.

156 The name is written simply Ia-aḫ-zu-^{d}ra-ša-ap. Three roots are apparently possible. As it is written, it would be from *ḪZʾ, which is unsure. [ub] or [ur] would give a form of ḪZB, "to rescue," or ḪZR, "to help." See Huffmon, Amorite Personal Names, 192-193.

157 Cited in Huffmon, Vattioni and Gelb, as in note 154.

158 For izi see Huffmon, Amorite Personal Names, 184-185, under WṢʾ; Roberts, Earliest Semitic Pantheon, 60, 65-66; and Moran, JAOS 90 (1970), 530b, izi = yaṣi, "Rešep goes out."

Gröndahl[159] and Nougayrol[160] read Rašap for Nergal in interpreting the logographic writings ^{d}MAŠ.MAŠ, ^{d}KAL and ^{d}GÌR.UNU.GAL.LA, as they occur in the Ras Shamra Akkadian texts. Gröndahl justifies this by noting that two of the logographically-written names are once spelled out syllabically. Not mentioned, but presumably underlying their reasoning is the fact that the equation Nergal = Rešep is well established. What is more, most of the names they cite in which Nergal occurs find exact parallels with ršp compound names in purely Ugaritic texts.

Gröndahl cites the following names: ^{d}rašap-a-bu/bi = Ug. ršpab(i), abdi-^{d}rašap/ra-ši-ip = Ug. ʿbdršp, aḫi (ŠEŠ)-^{d}rašap (^{d}MAŠ.MAŠ) = Ug. aḫršp, ili-^{d}rašap (^{d}MAŠ.MAŠ)/(GÌR.UNU.GAL.LA) = Ug. ilršp, and naʿam (SIG$_5$)-^{d}rašap (^{d}KAL) or nu-ma-re-ša-ip, "Rešep is gracious." The short text[161] in which the two names occur syllabically written is fragmentary and unrelated to the other texts. RS 16.145 is more suggestive, but not adequate to establish the thesis definitively.

In an Akkadian text from Ugarit,[162] a certain mār a-ri-iš-pi, "son of Arišpu," occurs, who is the father of aš-tar-a-bu. It is not certain whether or not his name contains the name of Rešep. In PRU III, 15.63, ^{1}ri-iš-pa-ia occurs four times.

Rešep appears as an element in a large number of personal names in Ugaritic texts.[163] Those which express a familial relationship with the god, or a relationship of servitude, are common forms in Semitic onomastica:[164] abršp,[165] ršpab,[166]

159 F. Gröndahl, Die Personennamen der Texts aus Ugarit [= Studia Pohl, 1] (Rome, 1967), 181 (and for passages cited here, 349, 317, 319, 326, 344 and 346 respectively.)

160 Passim in the Akkadian section of Ugaritica V.

161 Gröndahl does not cite the passages, but they both occur in RS 20.07, Ugaritica V, 191-192: nu-mar-re-ša-ip and abdi-ra-ša-ip. See also RS 16.145 from PRU III, 169, 12: abdi-ir-šap-pa, and 16: abdi-ir-šap. Further, see P. Matthiae, "Note sul dio siriano Rešef," OrAn 2 (1963), 35.

162 Text 16.134 in PRU III, 140. See also name list, 242.

163 In general, see Gröndahl, Die Personennamen, 181-182, and Vattioni, 43-45.

164 For a discussion of these, see A. Caquot, Syria 39 (1962), 238-242.

165 UT 321:I:35, 323:IV:6.

166 UT 300:5, 321:III:45, 1024:16, 1032:9, 1070:8, 1140:10, 2011:2, 2067:15, 2087:8, and perhaps 154:11. Also PRU V 11:2, 67:15, 87:8.

aḫršp,[167] (bn)[168] ršp(y),[169] ʿbd ršp,[170] and ršp mlk.[171] More interesting are ilršp,[172] ytršp,[173] ngršp,[174] and ʿdršp.[175] Gordon[176] and others[177] interpret the ytr- of ytršp as from W/YTR, and translate "Rešep is unique." This assumes, of course, that -r- = -rr-. Vattioni[178] cites PRU III, 202, 49: ya-tar-^{d}Nergal as convincing evidence that this is the case.

ngršp is more difficult. The element ng- occurs in other proper names.[179] Is it to be associated with *NWG(?), "depart," of Keret 131, 200? Another possibility is NGR, whence Akk. nagāru, Ug. ngr and Late Heb. naggar, "carpenter." To the best of my knowledge, no one has adverted to Arab. NJW, "to save, rescue," which might be a possibility.

Most commentators[180] agree that ʿdršp is probably "Rešep is eternal." As Gordon points out, "witness" is possible for ʿd, although Ugaritic already possesses the fairly common ypḥ with this meaning. It is not impossible that there is a root *ʿDR unrelated to ʿdr, "flock," which might be involved here. There is a (bn) ʿdr in UT 149:19 and UT 2034:B:3. Arabic has both ʿDR and ʿḎR, but the meanings are not suggestive.

167 UT 2067:7.

168 Is it possible that "bn" ršpy may refer to a class or profession of workers or artisans?

169 UT 64:12 (mdrġlm personnel), 1036:16 (list of craftsmen, "ḥršm"), 1047:9 (list of guards under the captaincy of pʿṣ), 301:II:17, 400:I:22, 1118:6, PRU V 68:12.

170 UT 1144:5, 2014:35.

171 UT 1106:58

172 Is -il "god" or El? See Caquot, Syria 39 (1962), 251.

173 UT 16:4. (A writing exercise? All names begin with y-), 301:I:11, 1024:24. Also attested are ytrhd (= -Hadd?), ytrʿm, ytršn.

174 UT 1125:Rev:2.

175 UT 1032:8, 1044:5, 1061:17, 1069:1, 1077:7, 1099:17, 2007:9, 2011:13.

176 UT, Glossary, No. 1170. For -rr- > -r- see Virolleaud, Syria 30 (1953), 188.

177 See references cited in Vattioni, 44.

178 Actually he cites line 35; apparently a misprint.

179 See UT, Glossary, No. 1605, and Vattioni, 44.

180 UT, Glossary, No. 1817; Vattioni, for other references.

Mention might be made here also of the early Fourth Century, B.C., inscriptions from Idalion and Kition in Cyprus,[181] where the proper name ršpytn is encountered. Ytn is a rather common onomastic element: mlkytn, pmyytn, bʿl-ytn, etc.

rb ršp as a proper name has also been reported in an Ammonite inscription.[182] The simple ršp as a proper name is only doubtfully attested in Ugaritic. ršp[. . .] occurs in UT 154:11 = PRU II 74:11[183] where the right side of the column is missing. In I Chron 7:25 the MT gives Rešep as one of the sons of Ephraim.[184]

Forrer[185] reported that in the Annals of Tiglath-Pileser III mention is made of a town Rašpūna, which he equated with the classical Apollonia, a site near Jaffa, a town whose name has survived as Arsûf. (A prothetic vowel such as in Arsûf is also affixed in the Hurrian form of Rešep, iršp = Iršippa.)[186] A subsequent examination of the cuneiform text, however, shows that the city-name in the Annals must be read Kašpūna instead of Rašpūna.[187]

B. REŠEP IN UGARITIC TEXTS

Compared to many other gods, Rešep's appearances in Ugaritic literature are few. It could be a mistake to pre-

181 G. A. Cooke, A Text-book of North-Semitic Inscriptions (Oxford, 1903) [Henceforth, Cooke, NSI], 23 = CIS I 88, and NSI 15 = CIS I 44. See also Vattioni, 45.

182 Aharoni in IEJ 1 (1950), 219-222; Vattioni, 45.

183 Vattioni, 45, lists UT 154:11 and PRU II 74:11 as two separate texts, but they actually are the same text.

184 LXX reads Raseph except for the Codex Vaticanus, which reads Saraph.

185 E. Forrer, Die Provinzeinteilung des Assyrischen Reiches (Leipzig, 1920), 60-61.

186 Larôche, Ugaritica V, 520-521, notes that initial r- is repugnant in Hurrian. He cites Hurro-Hittite argama-na- for Semitic *ragam-, "tribute." For iršp, see Ugaritica V, 520-521, and Larôche, JAOS 88 (1968), 150.

187 D. Wiseman in Iraq 13 (1951), 23 and Pl. XI, line 8.

dicate the relative importance of his role in the Ugaritic pantheon on this score alone, but such a factor certainly cannot be ignored.

In UT Keret 15-20 Rešep is the source of death for some of Keret's offspring--mḫmšt yitsp ršp, "one fifth (of them) Rešep gathered to himself"--and this is generally interpreted as a plague or pestilence.[188] In this role Rešep is, of course, much like Nergal, the Babylonian god of the underworld, master of plagues. This relationship between Rešep and Nergal has been handled at length in various studies,[189] and there is no need to pursue it here. It should be noted, however, that Nergal was also a god of warfare, and as such was often the patron of Assyrian kings in battle.[190] Particularly interesting is a passage in the epilogue to Hammurabi's Law Code,[191] where Nergal's role as god of pestilence and his role of god of warfare come together:

> "May Nergal, the strong one among the gods, the fighter without peer, who achieves victory for me, burn his [i.e., the enemy's] people in his great power, like the raging fire of swamp-reeds! May he cut him off with his powerful weapons, and break his body in pieces like an earthen image!"

Here Nergal's fierce role as destroyer is viewed as benevolent when he is conceived of as pitted against an enemy; the very factors which make him so awesome and fearful are an asset when he is taken on as a protector--much as Rešep in Egypt.

188 For translation problems, see Gaster, JQR 37 (1947), 289. For the problem of the numbers, see opinions in J. Gray, The KRT Text in the Literature of Ras Shamra, second ed. (Leiden, 1964), 32. (I find Gray's own opinion rather odd). Also Driver, "Ugaritic Problems," Studia Semitica Ioanni Bakoš Dicata (Bratislava, 1965), 95-96, and J. Finkel, "A Mathematical Conundrum in the Ugaritic Keret Poem," HUCA 26 (1955), 109-149.

189 Most recently in Conrad, ZAW 83 (1971), 158ff., where many other authors are cited. Vattioni, 54-55, cites interesting textual parallels. I might add "Nergal, lord of verdict, from whose presence the devils and plague creep into hiding," in E. Reiner, Šurpu: A Collection of Sumerian and Akkadian Incantations [= AfO Beiheft 11], 29, IV:100 and Commentary, 57. See now also E. von Weiher, Der babylonische Gott Nergal [= AOAT 11], (Neukirchen, 1971); for relationship between Nergal and Erra, also a plague god, see Roberts, Earliest Semitic Pantheon, 22-29.

190 See esp. ANET 277 (Shalmaneser III) and 311 (Nabonidus).

191 In ANET 180.

Nergal was known in Syria as early as 2000, B.C.[192] It is not surprising that Rešep, so similar to Nergal in his basic characteristics, would have come to be identified with him. That he was identified with him has now been explicitly established at Ugarit by comparative god-lists.[193] Seyrig[194] has also shown that in Hellenistic times Nergal was identified with Herakles in Syria, and Herakles' club became associated with Nergal. Now Bresciani[195] has published the torso of a male figure of the Hellenistic times whose provenance is evidently Lower Egypt. There are signs of the club over the shoulder remaining on the fragment, and this with the other anatomical features makes Bresciani's identification of the figure as Herakles virtually certain. Inscribed on the torso in Aramaic script of c. 250, B.C., is lršp mkl [. . .] ʿbdw[. . .,"to Rešep-MKL . . . ʿAbdu . . . ." Of MKL more later, but this association between Rešep and Herakles is significant. Elsewhere, as is well known, Rešep = Apollo.

Our next text is a most difficult one to interpret, UT 143, obverse:[196] btt ym ḥdt (2) ḫyr ʿrbt (3) špš tġrh (4) ršp. Dahood[197] translates: "during the six days of the new moon of the month of Ḫiyar the goddess Šapš sets, her porter being Rešep." The apparent astralization of Rešep in this text came as a surprise.[198] Aisleitner[199] avoided the ques-

192 See extensive lists of objects in Seyrig, Syria 24 (1945), 62-80, and remarks of Vattioni, 49. Nergal is mentioned in II Kgs 17:30, "the men of Cuth made [a statue of] Nergal." This is paralleled in the prologue of Hammurabi's Law Code, ii:68-iii:2 (ANET 165), "Erra [= Nergal] . . . who made Kutha preeminent."

193 See Larôche, "Notes sur le panthéon hourrite de Ras Shamra," JAOS 88 (1969), 150, and in Ugaritica V, 45, 57.

194 Seyrig, Syria 24 (1945), 62ff.

195 E. Bresciani, "Rešep-Mkl = Eracle," OrAn 1 (1962), 215ff.

196 The reverse reads w(ʿ?)bdm tbq(r?) skn. See PRU II, 190. Sawyer and Stephenson, BSOAS 33 (1970), 472ff., who consider the obverse to be an evil omen, suggest several translations for the reverse, favoring: "(This means that) the overlord will be attacked by his vassals."

197 M. Dahood, in S. Moscati, Ed., Le antiche divinità semitiche, 86. So also Virolleaud in PRU II, 189: "Pendant les six jours de la nouvelle lune du (mois de) Ḫiyar, elle se couche, la (déesse) Soleil, son portier (étant) Rešep."

198 For background on this in general, see Albright, "Gilgames and Engidu, Mesopotamian Genii of Fecundity," JAOS 40 (1920), 307-335, esp 328

tion by putting ršp with the reverse legend (whose translation remains highly problematic), and takes ʿrbt špš t̲ġrh as "die Sonne trat in ihre Türöffnung ein." Caquot[200] finds the astralization of Rešep an unacceptable interpretation, but Dahood objects:[201] "the astralization of Rešep may be much earlier than we suspect, and it is only a lack of documentation which prevents us from understanding the full and early Canaanite concept of Rešep."

I had originally shared Caquot's skepticism, but I am now convinced that Dahood is right after reading J. F. A. Sawyer and F. R. Stephenson, "Literary and Astronomical Evidence for a Total Eclipse of the Sun Observed in Ancient Ugarit on 3 May 1375 B.C."[202] While I have a bit of trouble with their translation, their evidence for their general interpretation is impressive, and better--they offer and document a reasonable context for the text, an eclipse. They translate: "The day of the new moon in the month of Hiyar was put to shame. The Sun went down (in the day-time) with

---

and 332-333; Albright, "Mesopotamian Elements in Canaanite Eschatology," Oriental Studies Published in Commemoration of the Fortieth Anniversary (1883-1923) of Paul Haupt (Baltimore, 1926), 143-154; Dahood in Moscati, Divinitá, 65-94, esp. 85ff.; A. Caquot, "Le dieu ʿAthtar et les textes de Ras Shamra," Syria 35 (1958), 45-60; Caquot, "La divinité solaire ougaritique," Syria 36 (1959), 90-101; also Dussaud in Archaeologia orientalia in memoriam E. Herzfeld (New York, 1952), 69-70, and Gray, PEQ 87 (1955), [Rešep = the planet Venus!]. Wider background in bibliographies in Albright JAOS 40 (1920), Caquot, Syria 35 (1958).

199 J. Aisleitner, AcOr 5 (1955), 22.

200 Caquot, Syria 35 (1958), 57: "Tout ce que nous savons du dieu Reshep ne permet pas d'en faire une divinité stellaire, cependent [le texte] nous montre un 'latastérisme' de Reshep, devenu le 'portier du soleil.'"

201 Dahood in Moscati, Divinità, 86-87: "Nor will it suffice to cite the katastérisme of Rešep who now appears in a Ugaritic text as a satellite of the Sun. It is true that up until now only very late texts have presented Rešep as a solar deity or as the Sun itself, and whom one identified as Apollo. But when we recall the conservative nature of Canaanite religion, we will not be surprised to find some of these late features also delineated in texts from the fourteenth century B.C. For example, in the fourth century Phoenician inscription of Eshmunazzar, ʿAt̲tart is described as the hypostasis of Baal, ʿt̲trt šm bʿl; and yet in the Keret legend (text 127:56), the exact same title of ʿAt̲tart is found. Hence the astralization of Rešep, etc." -- To this contrast the views of Vattioni, 47-48.

202 In BSOAS 33 (1970), 469-489.

Mars (= Rešep) in attendance." I refer the reader to their article for the details of their complex presentation.

The mention of Šapš and Rešep in a text referring to an eclipse--an event surely seen as an untimely "going down" of the sun--fits well into the general mythology surrounding Rešep. We know that in Mesopotamian mythology[203] the sun-god (UTU, Šamaš) descends at night into the sea, and spends the night wandering the underworld. There the sun-god brings light and food to the shades of the dead. Nergal here is host. (Nergal--or Erra or Gibil--as a fire-god is also the bringer of the sun's heat to mortals, but not, apparently as an astral deity.)

Just as Šamaš, as manifested by the nightly sojourn in the underworld, is "king of the shades"[204] in Mesopotamian mythology, so is the goddess Šapš the mistress of the dead in Ugaritic mythology.[205] We have noted in the Egyptian section of this study that šlm in the sense of "sunset" had a negative connotation of death. This may be due not only to the obvious connotation of the light of day disappearing, but also because the sun's setting is associated with entrance into the underworld.[206] I suggest that Rešep, like his underworld and plague-god counterpart, Nergal, is acting as host/attendant to Šapš in her descent or sudden disappearance into the underworld.

Let us move on now to other Ugaritic texts. Rešep is frequently listed together stereotypically with ʿAnat in various texts that involve groupings of gods.[207] This phenomenon has already been noted in regard to the so-called Turin Altar of Nectanebo II, E50. In UT 1, a list of sacrifices to various gods, we see the juxtaposition (1:7) [ʿ]nt š ršp

203 See Edzard in Haussig, Götter und Mythen under Sonnengott, 126.

204 CT XXXII, 18:38 = šar eṭimme.

205 See Astour, Hellenosemitica, 287-288 re UT 62:Rev:44b-49, and UT 128:V:18-20b. For rpim as "shades," see Caquot, "Les rephaim ougaritiques," Syria 37 (1960), 75-93.

206 See Aisleitner, AcOr 5 (1955), 7.

207 See esp. Gaster, "Groupings of Deities in the Ritual Tariffs from Ras Shamra-Ugarit," AfO 12 (1938/39), 148-150; Gaster, JQR 37 (1947), 287-288; B. Levine, "Ugaritic Descriptive Rituals," JCS 17 (1963), 105-111; Vattioni, 50-52.

š, "an animal[208] for ʿAnat, an animal for Rešep." The same formula appears in UT 3:16. In UT 128:II:6 there is this fragmentary section:

(1)	[ ]	[ ]
(2)	[ ] ṯr	[ ] the bull
(3)	[ali]yn bʿl	[mig]hty Baʿal
(4)	[ ]mn yrḫ zbl	[ ]mn princely Moon
(5)	[kṯ]r wḫss	[Koṯ]ar-and-Ḫasis
(6)	[ ] rḥmy ršp	[ ] Maiden and Rešep
(7)	[ʿ]dt ilm ṯlṯ	[as]sembly of the gods in (their) "tripartite division" (?)

There is little doubt that the "Maiden" is ʿAnat.[209] Gaster proposes[210] that three pairs of gods are involved, Baʿal and Yariḫ (Moon), X and Koṯar-and-Ḫasis, ʿAnat and Rešep, citing similar pairings in some ritual texts.[211] Elsewhere[212] Gaster sees Rešep and ʿAnat as the counterparts of Apollo and Artemis.[213]

Gaster[214] interprets the phrase aṯr bʿl as an epithet of ʿAnat, "ʿAnat, shrine of Baʿal." With this in mind he wishes to read UT 17:4, a[ ]r bʿl as aṯr bʿl, and notes that it is followed by ršp in the next line of this god-list. ʿAnat is also linked with Rešep in the comparative god-list we have already cited:[215] (12) iršp (13) ʿnt.

208 "Animal" is intentionally evasive. For discussion as to the exact meaning of š, see Levine, JCS 17 (1963), 108, and UT, Glossary, 2364.

209 See Gaster, JQR 37 (1947), 287.

210 Gaster goes a step further: "Baal and Yariḫ are gods of heaven; Rašap, the equivalent of Nergal, is a god of the netherworld; and Kôṯar is associated with the sea. Hence we may have the familiar tripartite division of the pantheon into supernatural, marine, and subterranean deities." (JQR 37 [1947], 287). This is not convincing. What of ʿAnat? Association with the sea does not strike me as one of Kothar's primary characteristics.

211 Besides Gaster, see also Gray, Keret, 58.

212 Gaster, AfO 12 (1938/39), 148. He also endorses the parallelism of Keraúnios/Keraúnia = Rešep/ʿAnat. See under Turin Altar, E50.

213 See also Gaster, Hellenosemitica, 56.

214 Gaster, AfO 12 (1938/39), 148, and in Studi Materiali di Storia della Religioni 12 (1936), 136. But see M. Pope, JBL 85 (1966), 458ff., for his comments on aṯr. Cf. also Astour, JNES 27 (1968), 21-22.

215 Ugaritica V, 520.

In UT 2004 there are two unusual expressions. In this ritual text enumerating sacrifices to gods, we find (10-11): k tʿrb ʿṯtrt šd bt [m]lk (11) k tʿrbn ršpm bt mlk, "when ʿAstarte of the Field enters the house of the king, when the Rešeps enter the house of the king." "ʿAstarte of the Field," paralleled in UT 1039:1 by bʿl šd, is difficult. There is not sufficient context to illuminate the use of the plural "Rešeps." Are they statues? Or, as Vattioni[216] suggests, "dei portieri"? Or is this a common plural, meaning collectively all the manifestations of Rešep?

In line 15 of the same text there is ršp ṣbi, "Rešep of the army/host."[216a] This epithet is reminiscent of the comparison made in the Medinet Habu text of Ramses III (E44): "They were as mighty as Rešeps." Reference must now be made to Miller[216b] who situates such epithets, both in Ugaritic literature and in the Old Testament, in the context of the lesser divinities who accompany the major deities out to battle.

ršp bbth appears in the "snake" text of Ugaritica V, RS 24.244. This text is frought with problems,[217] but it will suffice here to note that bbth in context, where a series of gods is listed with their city residences, could hardly mean "in his house," but must mean "at the city BBT." ršp bbt occurs in RS 24.249:11 (a list of sacrifices to gods at various tim s of the month), where "Rešep in his temple" might seem plausible were it not for ršp bbth in RS 24.244. Babtu would apparently be a city named after another divinity, and

216 Vattioni, 53. Dahood in Moscati, Divinità, 84, suggests "Statues of Rešep."

216a I resist the temptation to see ṣbi = ṣby, "gazelle." The Newsletter for Ugaritic Studies (CSBS/SBL) 10, April 1976, lists an article, M. Gilula, "ṣby in Isaiah 28:1 - A Head Ornament," Tel Aviv 1 (1974), 128, nothing that there is a reference to Rešep. I am not able to obtain this article in time to use here.

216b P. D. Miller, Jr., The Divine Warrior in Early Israel [= Harvard Semitic Monographs 5] (Cambridge, 1973), passim.

217 A. F. Rainey, "The Ugaritic Texts in Ugaritica V," JAOS 94 (1974), 189-190, surveys and evaluates the critical literature to date on this text, a most useful contribution. (Rainey objects to commentators citing texts from Ugaritica V by their RS numbers, preferring Gordon's UT equivalents. Admittedly, UT numbers would be more uniform, but when one has Ug. V open before him, RS numbers save a step or two.)

as Astour[218] remarks, "several ancient cities bore names of West Semitic goddesses, e.g., Ḫanat [= ʿAnat, modern ʿAnā] on the Euphrates, ʿAnātôt near Jerusalem, Aštartu in Transjordan, Baʿalat in Judah."

In the set of texts in Ugaritica V in which the two previous texts were published, Rešep appears in other intriguing contexts.[219] In RS 24.251:15, we find yrḫ and ršp linked together;[220] in a list of sacrifices to gods, RS 24.643: V 10, there is ršp idrp in a broken context. idrp is elsewhere unattested. Possible a place name? ršp in š[. .] or ršp inš[occurs in RS 24.271: B14. In RS 24.249:1 there is [b]ǵb ršp, where ǵb so far remains unexplained (Fisher: "cloud"),[221] and in line 10 of the same text, ršp mlk. From context it is not clear if mlk is genitive or an appositive.[222]

Among various sacrificial texts and others involving god-lists not yet mentioned, and in which ršp occurs without any significant qualifications, are RS 24.643:8, UT 1:4, UT 3:13, UT 1004:10, 11 and UT 144:8.[222a]

UT 1088 is a list of payments in silver to various shrines, one of which (line 3) is bt ršp gn, "the temple of Rešep of the garden," or "Rešep of the shield?"[223] Gordon[224] says: Vi-

218 Astour, JNES 27 (1968), 20. For a discussion of the goddess in question and the whole problem of [b]bt[h], see also Ugaritica V, 586 and 588; also Astour in JAOS 86 (1966), 283.

219 Again, see Rainey, JAOS 94 (1974), 184-194, for a discussion of several of these texts and for an up-to-date bibliography.

220 Ugaritica V, 576ff. The set of pairs is: il w ḥrn, bʿl w dgn, ʿnt w ʿṯtrt, yrḫ w ršp, ʿṯtr w ʿṯtpr, ṯṯ w kmṯ, (mlk b ʿṯtrt), kṯr w ḫss, šḥr w šlm.

221 The restoration seems certain. In the same text are bǵb ḫyr and bǵb ṣpn. See L. Fisher, Ras Shamra Parallels, II [= Analecta Orientalia 50], 142.

222 See Virolleaud's remarks, Ugaritica V, 592, and Fisher, RSP II, 142-143: npš w š l ršp bbt = "A man and a ram for the Ršp Bbt;" [b]ǵb ršpm p bnš = "[From] the cloud some Rešep-gods and a man;" ʿlm l ršp mlk = "In addition, for the Ršp mlk. . . ." See also Fisher in HTR 63 (1970), 485-501 on this text.

222a For discussion of these texts, see Schretter, Alter Orient, (cf. footnote 1 above), 117 - 119.

223 See S. Iwry, JAOS 81 (1961), 31, and Conrad, ZAW 83 (1971), 173-174.

224 UT, Glossary, 2356.

rolleaud informs me of a terra cotta lion's head with the following inscribed on its neck: pn arw d š'ly nrn l ršp gn, "the lion's face that N. has offered to R. of the garden.'"[225] However one interprets gn, the context surely implies that Rešep had a shrine or temple at Ugarit.

In UT 2005 Virolleaud restores r[ ]p in line 2 to read ršp ḥgb. The root ḤGB occurs in a number of Ugaritic personal names and also in the Old Testament.[226] There is a noun ḥagab in Lev 11:22 which is usually translated "grasshopper." The root also occurs in a few Babylonian names.[227] Virolleaud takes ḥgb as that which "saute en courant," and notes that Rešep is frequently associated iconographically with a gazelle-head. This does not seem a likely connections. I would see more likelihood in simply "Rešep the grasshopper," perhaps in relationship to the pestilential nature of locusts. Alternately there is the Arabic root ḤJB, "to veil or screen off," whence ḥijâba, "office of gate-keeper, and ḥâjib, "doorman, gate-keeper." This would fit nicely the reference to Rešep in UT 143 as tġr špš.[228]

Finally, there is UT 1001:3, b'l ḥẓ ršp. Allow me to defer discussion of this until we mention the Cypriot inscription where ršp ḥṣ is encountered.

C. PHOENICIAN AND ARAMAIC INSCRIPTIONS

Rešep occurs in a number of inscriptions from the Eight to the Third Centuries, B.C. The contexts are as varied as the locations from which they emanate. Most have had a thorough discussion in the literature.

Probably the earliest of these is the Aramaic inscription of Panammuwa I,[229] middle Eighth Century, B.C. from

225 See further discussion in Vattioni, 45.

226 See Ezra 2:45, 46 and Neh 7:48. Also Conrad, ZAW 83 (1971), 179; PRU V, 12.

227 UT, Glossary, 836.

228 According to Du Mesnil du Buisson, Études sur les dieux phéniciens hérités par l'Empire Romain (Leiden, 1970), xvii, Caquot related ḥgb to Arabic ḥâjib.

229 Cooke, NSI 61 = Donner-Röllig, KAI, 214.

Zinjirli in northern Syria. The pertinent portions of the inscription read: " (2) the gods Hadad, El, Rešep, Rākib-El and Šamaš stood by me, and Hadad, El, Rākib-El, Šamaš and Rešep (3) put into my hand the scepter of ḥlbbh; and Rešep stood by me. . . . (11) and Hadad, El, Rākib-El, Šamaš and Arqrešep (ʾrqršp) provided abundantly, and gave me greatness."

What is particularly notable is the evidently high station Rešep enjoyed in the pantheon of Zinjirli. In (2) he is listed after Hadad--the inscription is on a statue of Hadad--and El, but the order given in (3) and (11), after Rākib-El and Šamaš, might be more indicative. There is no discernible reason why Rešep is singled out in (3), unless other gods were mentioned in the lacuna following.

ʾrqršp is a problem. From context it seems clear that ʾrqršp = ršp, but whatever its meaning, it is strange that he should be called this after twice being called ršp. Is ʾrqršp conceivably for ʾrṣ-ršp, ʾrṣ being the god identified with the Evening Star, known from Palmyra and Dura Europos? Albright[230] opposes this view, arguing that, if anything, Rešep would be more akin to ʿAzîz, the Morning Star, Arṣu's opposite. He prefers the interpretation that ʾrqršp = "Land of Rešep," as in the Sidonian inscription, KAI 15.[231] He says, "[this] shows that the Syrians did not draw a clear distinction at the time between the god and his sphere of influence." Vattioni[232] rightly rejects this interpretation but offers no alternate suggestion.[233]

Actually, there is more to be said for the identification ʾrq = Arṣu than Albright was able to point out in his early article. It may be true that Arṣu, who equalled Venus, was a feminine deity (= Ruḍâʾ) for the Arabs, but the fact remains that at Palmyra Arṣu was a masculine deity. Furthermore, study of the Rešep-Šulman stele and Rešep's relation-

230 Albright, Studies for Paul Haupt, 147-148, n. 4. See Höfner in Haussig, Götter und Mythen, 426.

231 See also KAI, Kommentar, 24.

232 Vattioni, 57.

233 J. C. L. Gibson, Textbook of Syrian Semitic Inscriptions, II: Aramaic Inscriptions (Oxford, 1975), 71, wants "favourite of Resheph," passive partic. with prosthetic [ʾ], cf. rṣwy in Deut 33:24.

ship to Nergal, specifically as a god who welcomes the sun into the underworld at night, shows that to link Rešep with a god of the evening is not at all inappropriate. If the interpretation of Rešep (who is twice in this inscription linked with Šamaš) as the ṯġr špš is correct as we have stated it earlier, the identification between Rešep and Arṣu is strongly reinforced.

There has already been considerable discussion in the literature of ršp ṣprm in the Karatepe Phoenician and Hieroglyphic Hittite bilingual inscription of c. 720, B.C.[234] On the face of it ṣprm would seem to mean either "birds" or "he-goats." Opinion has been strongly in favor of the second option, largely because of Rešep's association with the gazelle in Egypt, and because the corresponding Hittite hieroglyph depicts a stag or some other antlered animal.

I. Levi,[235] followed by Solâ Solê[236] and Vattioni,[237] makes a more plausible proposal: a city-name underlies ṣprm. This suggestion draws greater weight insofar as the other frequently-mentioned god of the Karatepe text is bʿl krntrys/š, the second word being evidently the name of an Anatolian city (I suggest nearby Kelenderis) which must have had a particularized cult of Baʿal. There are two texts in PRU III[238] liberally sprinkled with non-Semitic (Anatolian?) names which speak of the locality Sippiru (ṣi-ip-pi-ru), in each case associated, at least indirectly, with a certain ʿAbdi-Nergal. It is quite possible that Ṣippiru was a town in the Cilician area which had a special cult of Rešep.

Whatever one decides on ṣprm--I opt for a place-name--it is clear that at Karatepe Rešep played a positive role and was looked on as a special patron of Azitawaddiya. Furthermore, as at Zinjirli, he seemed to have enjoyed a prominent place in the local pantheon.

A cippus from Palaeo-Kastro in Cyprus, which Caquot

234 KAI 26, where further bibliography is given.

235 I. Levi, in Bulletin de l'Académie royale de Belgique, Classe de Lettres 39 (1953), 297ff. Levi suggests an identification with the Sepyra mentioned in Cicero, Ad Fam. XV, 4, 7-9.

236 Solâ Solê, Sefarad 16 (1956), 353.

237 Vattioni, 56.

238 PRU III 16:157 (pp. 83-84), 16.250 (pp. 85-86).

and Masson[239] date to the Seventh Century, B.C, by its paleography, has this fragmentary inscription: ʾš pʿl ʾšmnḥlṣ hqlʿ lʾdny lršpš[. Lacau[240] translates: "Ce qu'a fait Eshmounhilleç, le frondeur, à son seigneur, à Reshef de Sh[." ʾšmnḥlṣ is encountered elsewhere in Phoenician, once in an inscription from Spain (KAI 72), once from Carthage (KAI 73) and, according to Caquot and Masson,[241] in another inscription from Cyprus. For ršpš[, Caquot and Masson suggest ršp šmm, ršp šm (citing ʿštrt šm in CIS I 3:18 as parallel), or ršp šr, but of course this is guesswork. This inscription is the earliest from Cyprus to mention Rešep.

The Fifth Century, B.C., inscription (KAI 15) of Bōdʿaštart from Sidon has the following: ". . .in 'Sidon of the Sea,' 'the High Heaven,' 'the Land of the Rešeps (ʾrṣ ršpm).'" The epithet for Sidon, "Land of the Rešeps," occurs in other Sidonian inscriptions.[242] Only once[243] is it in the singular, ʾrṣ ršp. Vattioni[244] rejects the idea that we are here dealing with a plurale magnitudinis of Rešep, and suggests "terra dei lampi" as a translation. It is not clear if he considers this an impersonal usage of a root *RŠP or a personification (in the form of Rešep[s]) of lightening flashes. As will be seen, I have problems with both ideas, and would prefer the general meaning "Land of the Warriors."

From Ibiza in Spain comes a Fifth Century inscription[245] mentioning ršp mlqrt: lʾdn lʾršp mlqrt mqd[š] z ʾš ndr ʾšʾdr bn ʿš[ ] bn brgd bn ʾšmnhlṣ. The prothetic aleph is sufficiently common in Punic[246] that ʾršp for ršp causes no problem. There is also a seal[247] found at Tyre which reads:

239 Caquot and Masson, "Deux inscriptions phêniciennes de Chypre," Syria 45 (1968), 295ff.

240 In Caquot and Masson, Syria 45 (1968), 298.

241 In Syria 45 (1968), 298.

242 RES 289:2, 290:3, 302 B:5.

243 RES 294:3.

244 Vattioni, 61.

245 KAI 72 A. With old editions, see corrections, III, 82.

246 See Z. Harris, A Grammar of the Phoenician Language (New Haven, 1936), 33.

247 M. A. Levy, Siegel und Gemmen (Breslau, 1869), 31, no. 18.

lbʿlytn ʾš ʾlm lmlqrt rṣp, "To Baʿalyaton, a man of the god/gods, who belongs to Melqart-RṢP." Cooke[248] dates this inscription to the Fifth or Fourth Century. Although very odd, it has been generally agreed[249] that rṣp = ršp, and that this inscription parallels that from Ibiza. There is a possibility that rṣp could be a city, however.[250] Lipinski[250a] takes it as a passive participle of *RṢP (cf. Cant 3:10), and suggests "(Belonging) to Baal-yaton, the man of God, who is firmly attached to Melqart." I do not find this convincing.

Dussaud[251] interprets mlqrt-rṣp as "Melqart (the son of) Rešep." He does not comment on Ibiza's ʾršp-mlqrt. Vattioni[252] rejects this view, pointing to the very common assimilation and virtual identification of various gods in the late Phoenician-Punic world. Röllig[253] sees Melqart's association with Rešep linked with the fact that a perpetual fire burnt before Melqart's altar.

If Rešep and Melqart were associated only in Spain, one could reasonably suspect that the phenomenon was due to the syncretism following upon the imposition of a Phoenician religion on a foreign people far from the homeland. The fact that the association occurs at Tyre, however, even if at a relative late date, complicates the question.

Seyrig[254] has explored the association of Nergal, Herakles and Melqart, the god of Tyre, in Syria. His arguments

248 Cooke, NSI 361, no. 5.

249 Levy, Siegel und Gemmen, 31; Cooke, NSI 361; KAI, Kommentar, 89; Vattioni, 65; Harris, Grammar, 147.

250 See entries under RṢP in Koehler-Baumgartner, Lexicon.

250a In Revista de Studi Fenici II/1 (1974), 54-55.

251 R. Dussaud, "Melqart," Syria 25 (1946), 229.

252 Vattioni, 65. Donner and Röllig, KAI, Kommentar, 88-89, distinguishes four categories of compound divine names: (1) those combining a divine name, usually as a bʿl, with a city-name, such as bʿl ṣdn, bʿl ṣr, ʿštrt pp, etc.; (2) those combining a god's name with an appropriate symbol, as bʿl ṣmd, ršp ḥṣ, etc.; (3) those modifying the god's name with an adjective or participle, bʿl ʾdr, ʾšmn mʾrḥ, etc.; and (4), which becomes progressively more frequent in later times through syncretism, ršp mlk, mlqrt ʾšmn, even ʾšmn ʿštrt and mlk ʿštrt.

253 Röllig in Haussig, Götter und Mythen, 298.

254 Seyrig, Syria 24 (1944/45), 62ff. Dussaud, Syria 25 (1946), 226, would qualify Seyrig's views.

concerning the basis of this identification,[255] particularly between Melqart and Nergal, are not particularly cogent, but the fact of the identification seems hard to deny, and it is likely that it is in this area that the question of Rešep = Melqart is to be pursued. Unfortunately, despite the fairly large corpus of materials relating to Melqart, not enough has been determined of his history and characteristics to make a definitive statement in this matter. Suffice it to note that in the Fifth Century Rešep had found his way to Spain and evidently had important cult there. Some would even wish to see Rešep in various figurines and seals from the Ibiza area,[256] but as with the ubiquitous "Rešep-bronzes," this can remain only a conjecture.

We now come to a set of inscriptions from Cyprus which are of the highest interest because of the epithets they attach to Rešep. The first of these is from Kition, datable to 341, B.C.,[257] the dedication of an altar and two hearths to *ršp-ḥṣ*. The problem of *ršp-ḥṣ* found new grist with the publication of a very fragmentary Ugaritic text[258] in which this occurs:]*t bʿl ḥẓ ršp.*[259]

One early suggestion[260] was that *ḥṣ* = Heb. *ḥûṣ*, "outside," and *ršp ḥṣ* = something like "Rešep of the street." By far the most popular view has been to take *ḥṣ* as the Heb. *ḥēṣ*, "arrow," and precisely in the sense of a weapon, not as an instrument of divinization or as a charm.[261]

This view has much in its favor. Rešep was a war-god

255 Seyrig, *Syria* 24 (1944/45), 71ff.

256 See in Vattioni, 65.

257 *CIS* I 10, *NSI* 12, *KAI* 32.

259 This phrase is followed by *b-km.yr.* Virolleaud, *PRU II*, 5, reads *bn* for *b-*, but the reading is very doubtful. From the photograph, it may well be a single horizontal stroke = *t*. If the reading is *bn*, is there here an epithet of Rešep? On the meaning of *km.yr* (*kmyr*), see summary of opinions in Gray, *Keret*, 41. In *Krt* 92-93, *kmyr* is parallel with *ḫdd*. If *ḫdd* = *ḥazîz*, "storm-cloud," perhaps *yôreh*, "early rain," should be seen in (*km*)*yr*.

260 Clermont-Ganneau, *Recueil d'archéologie oriental* I (1888), 176ff. Also Harris, *Grammar*, 104.

261 *Passim* in the earlier writings of Albright; also Dahood in Moscati, *Divinità*, 84.

who is naturally associated with weapons, and in at least three instances,[262] Rešep wears a quiver-full of arrows in Egyptian representations. Furthermore, Rešep is consistently identified with Apollo in Cyprus inscriptions, the archer in Greek mythology, Apóllôn hekêbólos, "Apollo the far-shooter." Indeed, Apollo's skill with the arrow is associated with his capacity for bringing plagues, as the opening lines of the Iliad vividly describe. One description of Apollo (I:45ff.) would be very consistent with the image of Rešep:[263]

> "Down he strode, wroth at heart, bearing on his shoulders his bow and covered quiver. The arrows rattles on the shoulders of the angry god as he moved; and his coming was like the night. Then he sat down apart from the ships and let fly a shaft; terrible was the twang of his silver bow. The mules he assailed first and the swift dogs, but thereafter on the men themselves he let fly his stinging arrows, and smote; and ever did the pyres of the dead burn thick."

This onslaught was, of course, a plague. One is immediately reminded of the fate of Keret's sons at the hands of Rešep, and of the various attacks of fever and disease let loose by Rešep's Mesopotamian counterpart, Nergal.[264]

Despite this impressive iconographic and literary evidence, S. Iwry, in an article which it has become de rigueur to cite,[265] maintains that ršp ḥṣ is not "Rešep of the arrow (in the sense of a weapon)," but "Rešep of luck," and in this he had convinced Albright,[266] who repudiated his own earlier position. For arrow = luck, Iwry builds an excellent case for widespread belomancy in the ancient Near East. Philologically, he cites the direction ḥṣ(ṣ)/ḥẓ(ẓ) has taken in Arbic, where ḥaẓẓa means "to be lucky." Gordon[267] agrees with this extension of the root's semantic range. Texts they

262 E22, E39, E46.

263 From Loeb Iliad (Cambridge, 1945), trans. A. Murray, 7.

264 See striking passages in Deut 32:23-24, Ps 78:48.

265 S. Iwry, "New Evidence for Belomancy in Ancient Palestine and Phoenicia," JAOS 81 (1961), 27-34.

266 Albright, Yahweh and the Gods of Canaan (Garden City, N Y., 1968), 139; also Albright, The Proto-Sinaitic Inscriptions and their Decipherment, second ed., (London, 1969), 49, under "Additional Notes for the Second Edition."

267 Gordon, UT, Glossary, 853-854.

both cite are UT 51:IV:42 and UT ʿnt:V:39, parallels: tḥmk il ḥkm ḥkmt ʿm ʿlm ḥyt ḥẓt tḥmk. Translators have been fairly unanimous in their handling of the adjectival ḥẓt: Albright: "Thy command, O El, is wise, thy kingdom lasts forever, a life of good fortune is thy command;"[268] Gordon: ". . .lucky life is thy word;"[269] Gaster: " . . .mayest thou thrive and prosper forever;"[270] Ginsberg: ". . .ever life is thy portion."[271] There seems little doubt that some such meaning is behind ḥẓt in this context. Unfortunately, however, the simple ḥẓ has yet to appear in a similar context!

Since ḥẓ is certainly attested in Ugaritic with the meaning of "arrow" as a weapon, and since this is the normal meaning of ḥṣ in Hebrew, and since "Rešep of the arrow" fits ideally with the other evidence,[272] I believe "Rešep of luck" should be disregarded.

Finally, it should be noted that several commentators who espouse the translation "Rešep of the arrow" suggest "Rešep of the lightening(-bolt)" as an alternative.[273] This idea seems to be based partly on the supposed connotation of "burning" in a hypothetical root RŠP, partly on certain Old Testament passages, and probably on the old view that Rešep was a weather-god. This last idea stems in part from the so-called "Rešep-bronzes" and the related "Hadad-bronzes." In light of the above, this suggestion should also be abandoned.

In four inscriptions from Idalion in Cyprus, one of them a bilingual, ršp mkl is encountered. Probably the oldest is CIS I 90,[274] dated to 391, B.C., in which Milkyaton of Idalion dedicates an object to "his god, ršp-mkl in Idalion." The second[275] is similar in content, but has a Cyp-

268 Albright, in Festschrift Alfred Bertholet (Tübingen, 1950), 5.

269 Gordon, Ugaritic Literature (Rome, 1949), 32.

270 Gaster, Thespis, rev. ed., Harper ppbk. (New York, 1961), 184.

271 Ginsberg in ANET, 133.

272 Similarly, if the words bʿl ḥṣ ršp go together, the translation would be something like "the master of the arrow, Rešep."

273 E.g., Pope in Haussig, Götter und Mythen, 305, and KAI, Kommentar, 50-51.

274 KAI 38 = NSI 24.

275 CIS I 89 = KAI 39.

riot Greek version, wherein corresponding to ršp mkl is to a-po-lo-ni a-mu-ko(?)-lo-i = tôi Apollôni Amuklôi, i.e., "(to) Apollo Amyklos" or "(to) Apollo of Amyclae." ršp mkl also appears in an inscription of 255, B.C.[276]

We have already mentioned a torso of Herakles with the inscription lršp mkl. Caquot and Masson have recently published yet another inscription from Idalion,[277] similar to the others, but this time with the definite article prece- mkl: lʾly lršp hmkl, "to his god, to Rešep (the) mkl."

There is another Cyprus bilingual text,[278] from Tamassos, dating to 363, B.C., in which Rešep is likewise identified with an Apollo of a local cult: [rš]p ʾlyyt = to-i a-pe-i-lo-ni to-i e-le-i-ta-i = tôi Apeilôni tôi Eleitai, Apollo of Helos. There is a similar inscription from Tamassos[279] where ršp ʾlhyts = a-po-lo-ni a-la-si-o-ta-i. There is some disagreement as to the identification of a-la-si-o-ta-i,[280] but there seems little doubt that ʾlhyts/a-la-si-o-ta-i is a city-name, and that again Rešep of City X = Apollo of the same City X.

But what of mkl and Amyklae? Earlier commentators considered that this was another case of city = city. Amyklae could not be readily identified, but some[281] suggested a city of that name in Laconia. Cooke[282] explained the mkl with no corresponding initial vowel as an attempt by the Phoenicians to adapt a foreign word to a triliteral form familiar to them.

The situation was made considerably more complex by a find made at Beisan in 1927, an Egyptian stele (E52) devoted

276 CIS I 93 = KAI 40 = NSI 27.

277 Caquot and Masson, "Deux inscriptions phéniciennes de Chypre," Syria 45 (1968), 302ff. Noteworthy in this inscription, besides the article with mkl, are z for ʾz, and again, the article with sml,--hsml.

278 RES 1212 = KAI 41 = NSI 30.

279 RES 1213. See also Vattioni, 59.

280 See discussion in Vattioni, 59-60.

281 See KAI, Kommentar, 56; Astour, Hellenosemitica, 311.

282 Cooke, NSI 76. The form hmkl raises problems, however. If the meaning were "of Amyklae," the article would be unexpected. If it were a gentilic, one would expect a nisbe, hmkly. If hmkl involves a participle, it is difficult to determine which it would be.

to the theretofore unknown god mkl.[283] In the upper register mkl sits enthroned, a wꜣs-scepter in his left hand, an ʿankh in his left. He has a high conical hat from which two streamers hang, and on the front are two thin horns. Before him are the architect Amen-em-opet and his son. In the lower register is the dedicatory inscription. mkl's name occurs in the center of the upper register: mʿkꜣr, the full spelling indicating a non-Egyptian name.

The literature dealing with this mkl and ršp mkl is vast and I have no new suggestions, just a strong opinion. Whatever the meaning of mkl--a participial form is the most common opinion[284]--is it this god's name which underlies the mkl of ršp mkl in Cyprus, even if the Greek parallel, Amuklos/Amyklae, refers to a city? Is ršp mkl a compound name such as ršp-šlmn or ršp-mlqrt, representing the identification of two gods?[285] I believe that mkl is simply a local epithet for another god, possibly Seth,[286] and that there is no such

283 ANEP 487, discussion in ANET 249. See now especially H. O. Thompson, MEKAL: The God of Beth-Shan (Leiden, 1970). This book has a special chapter on Rešep, and one on mkl in Cyprus = Rešep. Although the book is loaded with useful references, the author--in my opinion--seems to assimilate the view of virtually everybody to the point where by logic they become mutually exclusive, and apart from the excellent archaeological part of the book, I find the book confused. To one degree or another Thompson identifies Rešep with Baʿal, Môt, Hadad, Adonis, Šulman, Melqart, Herakles, Nergal, Apollo, and of course, mkl.

284 Caquot and Masson, Syria 45 (1968), 311, suggest *mʾkl > mkl, "le devorant." They cite other suggestions, forms of the roots KWL and KLY. See now also Thompson, MEKAL, 188-192, and Conrad, ZAW 83 (1971), 164-169. Vincent, RB 37 (1928), 525-528, took the god's name as a derivative of YKL, and suggested that he was the "Conquering one." Albright's complicated proposal, BASOR 90 (1943), 33, which has not gained wide acceptance, would have Sum. Urugâlla(k) (from Nergal's epithet Umun-urugâlla[k], which he translates "lord of the great city") > *Muk(k)alla. As Astour, Hellenosemitica, 311, points out, "it requires us to postulate the elision of too many vowels and especially consonants." Astour's own proposal is not noteworthy. He suggests that Sum. GIŠ.GAL, "great tree," would be MU.GAL in the Emesal dialect, and MU.GAL > Mugalla > Mûkal = mkl. See also now Schretter, Alter Orient, 158-170.

285 Vattioni, 58, finds this difficult in light of ršp hmkl: "La presenza dell' articolo precisa per la prima volta che mkl è un aggettivo qualificato di ršp e lascia pensare che tale epiteto può essere diventato un nome divino a meno che non si tratti di un accostamento con un' altra divinità come nel caso di Resheph-Melqart."

286 Albright, BASOR 90 (1943), 33-34.

god mkl on his own right. If he were such a god, it would be very surprising that we have no other attestation of his existence. Even more unlikely would be Albright's[286] hypothesis that his cult was sufficiently popular so as to travel westward from Beisan to Cyprus, let alone to the Greek mainland where a city Amyclae was named after him!

Although mkl in Cyprus may have been inspired by the knowledge that that epithet was applied to a god in Palestine, I will throw in my lot with Stadelmann and with Caquot and Masson:

> "Viel näher schient hier eine Erklärung auf Grund der lautspielerischen Ähnlichkeit der Namen mkl und Amyclai zu liegen;"[287] --- "Le syncrétisme institué à Chypre--et à Chypre seulement--entre Reshef et Apollon explique que le titre de mkl ait été rendu au moyen de noms propres présentant avec lui une certaine homonymie, Amyklos ou Amuklaîos, qui pouvaient en même temps convenir comme épithètes d'Apollon."[288]

D. REŠEP AT CARTHAGE, BYBLOS

A large number of Near Eastern deities were honored at Carthage as that city moved into Roman times: Melqart, Ešmun, ʿAstarte, Yam, Dagan and others.[289] Rešep apparently had a temple, to judge by ʿbd bt ʾrš[p] in CIS I 251. (Note the prothetic aleph, not surprising in Punic.) The proper name ʿbdršp also occurs (CIS 2628).

Apollo had a notable cult at Carthage, and there has been considerable speculation that Apollo is a Hellenization of Rešep.[290] This is plausible, but sometimes authors[291] speak of a widespread cult of Rešep at Carthage when properly they should speak of a cult of Apollo, whom they assume--with good reason--to be identified with Rešep in Carthage, just as in Cyprus.

287 Stadelmann, Gottheiten, 53.

288 Caquot and Masson, Syria 45 (1968), 312-313.

289 See D. Harden, The Phoenicians (New York, 1963), 86ff., and Vattioni, 62-63.

290 Vattioni, 63, assembles the various Carthaginian items of evidence relating to Apollo.

291 E.g., Gese et alii in Die Religionen Altsyriens, Altarabiens und der Mandäer (Stuttgart, 1970), 205ff.; also Harden, The Phoenicians, 86ff.

Similarly, the "Temple of Rešep" at Byblos is actually a temple associated with Ḥerišef ([H]arsaphes), the Egyptian god of Herakleopolis,[292] whom some authors believe is, at least at Byblos, actually Rešep. Rešep, as we noted in the Egyptian section of this study, may also have been associated with Herakleopolis. But it is annoying to read such unqualified statements as this of Gese:[293] "Aus einer Inschrift des Stadtfürsten Abischmuʿ geht hervor, dass dieser Tempel dem Rešep geweiht war." Checking his reference to Dunand,[294] one finds, of course, Ḥerišef, not Rešep.[295]

Once Gese has "established" that Rešep had a thriving cult at Byblos (based on the Ḥerišef inscription), he moves to "Allem Anschein nach ist der Rešepkult von Byblos in der Spätzeit in einem Adoniskult übergegangen, wobei Rešep den Todesaspekt des Adonis repräsentiert."[296] And again:[297] "Vielleicht hatte Rešep worher wesentliche Seiten der Vegetationsfunktion Baʿals als Motgestalt mit übernommen." Zounds!

292 Cf. Helck in Haussig, Götter und Mythen, 355 (Harsaphes).

293 In Die Religionen Altsyriens, etc., 46.

294 M. Dunand, Fouilles de Byblos (Paris, 1948), II, 878, no. 16980. See also discussion by P. Montet, Kêmi 16 (1962), 89-90.

295 So Du Mesnil du Buisson, Études, 63-64, "Ḥerishef (ḥršf) était un dieu égyptien, seigneur de Nen-nesou, chef-lieu du XXe nome de la Haute Égypte, mais il est évident que dans les inscriptions émanant de princes asiatiques, aussi bien à Tanis qu'ici, ce nom ne représente pas cette divinité locale égyptienne mais, par à peu près, un dieu sémitique bien connu: Réshéf." His reference again turns out to be a text dealing with Ḥerišef (Leclant and Yoyotte, Kemi 14 [1957], 52-54), and he presents no evidence that this divinity is Rešep in disguise. Du Mesnil du Buisson quite misinterprets Leclant and Yoyotte's discussion of the hieroglyphic "determinative" involved in the Ḥerišef inscription. As to the assertion that the Byblians had Rešep in mind even when they wrote Ḥerišef, enough has been said about the impossibility of using these bronzes as if their association with Rešep were a certainty.

296 Gese in Die Religionen Altsyriens, 143. He says earlier (142): "Eine grosse Rolle scheint der Rešepkult in Byblos gespielt zu haben, wo der Obeliskentempel dem Rešep geweiht war, warschienlich auch der Vorläufer dieses Tempels."

297 Gese, 143.

E. REŠEP IN THE OLD TESTAMENT

Rešep (or "the Rešeps") occurs seven times in the Old Testament.[298] If contemporary translators are at a loss as to how to handle these passages, the ancient versions provide a no less chaotic array of interpretations.

The immediate context of Deut 32:23-24 in the Song of Moses is a recitation of the evils Yahweh will visit on those who are unfaithful to him: ʾsph ʿlymw rʿwt ḥṣy ʾklh-bm mzy rʿb wlḥmy ršp wqṭb mryry wšn bhmwt ʾšlḥ bm ʿm ḥmt zḥly ʿpr, "I will heap(?)[299] evils upon them, my arrows I will spend on them, empty(?) with hunger and assailed (devoured?)[300] by Rešep and poisonous Qeṭeb. I will send against them the fangs of beasts, with the venom of creatures that creep in the dust." The RSV translates 24a: "They shall be wasted with hunger and devoured with burning heat and poisonous pestilence." From the Jerusalem Bible: "For weapons I shall have barns of famine, fever and consumption for poison."

Caquot[301] suggests that ršp and qṭb be translated as proper names and considered demons. To Caquot the versions seem to conceive of plagues as preternatural figures, here specifically winged creatures who snatch away life.[302] One is reminded of the winged creature of the Cassirer scarab (E14) which can, however, only with difficult be associated

298 Deut 32:24; I Chron 7:25 (as a proper name: Rešep, son of Ephraim), Ps 76:4, Ps 78:48, Job 5:7, Cant 8:6, and Hab 3:5.

299 ʾsph is difficult. MT has ʾaspeh < SPH, Hifʿil. Possibly ʾosipāh < YSP.

300 "Devoured" is more traditional, but "assail, embattle" is not only possible, but perhaps desirable here. See Caquot, "Sur quelques dêmons de l'Ancien Testament (Reshep, Qeṭeb, Deber)," Semitica 6 (1956), 59, notes 1 and 2. Also Vattioni, 68; and esp. N. Tromp, Primitive Conceptions of Death and the Nether World in the Old Testament (Rome, 1969), 108, n. 43.

301 Caquot, Semitica 6 (1956), passim, esp. 59. See also Vattioni, 68. The ancient versions almost unanimously translate ršp as "bird(s)." For (mzy rʿb) wlḥmy ršp, LXX has (tēkómenoi limôi kai) brōsei ornéōn, "(wasted with famine and) the eating of birds," while the Vulgate reads "et eos devorabunt aves." Aquila reads bebrōménoi ptēnôi, and Onkelos, ʾakūlē ʿūp, "eaten by birds." The Peshitta, however, has "the pang of hunger, the fever of heat."

302 Caquot, Semitica 6 (1956), 55.

with Rešep.[303]

qṭb is a rare word in the Old Testament.[304] The root *QṬB apparently means "to cut off," and its noun-form has been translated "sting," "disease," "plague." In Late Hebrew tradition Qeṭeb and Rešep are demons.[305]

Hab 3 describes the upheavals of nature that typically accompany a theophany.[306] We read in vv. 3-4:

> "God came from Teman, and the Holy One from Mount Paran. His glory covered the heavens, and the earth was full of his praise. His brightness was like the light, rays flashed from his hand; and there he veiled his power (?)."

The text continues, lpnyw ylk dbr wyṣ' ršp lrglyw, "Before him goes Deber (plague); Rešep follows on his heels." Both Caquot and Vattioni[307] interpret Deber and Rešep here as mythological figures, lesser divinities who accompany Elohim as natural forces at his command. Both cite 1 Sam 5 as a parallel, where the presence of the Ark of God amongst the enemy Philistines brings death and disease.[308] Miller[309]

303 Caquot takes the ršp sprm of the Karatepe inscription as "Rešep of the birds." Even if that were correct--which I question--the image would not seem to be the same as what Caquot suggests for Deut 32:24 where Rešep himself is a démon ailé.

304 See Hos 13:14, Is 28:2, Ps 91:6.

305 See under QṬB and RŠP in Jastrow, Dictionary. In Berakot, 52, referring to Deut 32:24, Rešep is an "evil spirit."

306 See examples in Jgs 4:4; Pss 18:8, 68:8, 77:19, 97:4; Is 6:4; Mi 1:4; Nah 1:5; Ezk 1:4; Deut 33:2, et al. The theophany of Hab 3 seems to be the only one to include disease or plague, if, indeed, we are to interpret ršp and dbr as such here.

307 Caquot, Semitica 6 (1956), 57-58; Vattioni, 67-68. Is Deber also an underworld divinity? See UT 49:II:19:19-20 where arṣ dbr seems to be part of the realm of Môt. Recall the unsavory characters who reside in the Mesopotamian underworld as Nergal's minions.

308 Vattioni notes the similarity between the Hab text and the Adad-theophany in the eleventh tablet of Gilgamesh (ANET 94): "With the first glow of dawn, a black cloud rose over the horizon. Inside it Adad thunders, while Shullat and Hanish go in front, moving as heralds over hill and plain." The characterization of Šullat and Ḫaniš cannot, unfortunately, be determined aside from this context.

The ancient versions here do not support the interpretation of Rešep and Deber as mythological figures, a fact which Caquot explains as the effort of the early translators to demythologize a statement in the sacred text which they found religiously embarrassing. LXX reads dbr as lógos, reading dābār, whereas MT has dāber. It substitutes en pedílois for ršp,

has now shown that in both these instances we are dealing with the typology of the divine warrior accompanied by his army.

The reference to Rešep in Job 5:7 is particularly difficult. In a set of aphorisms stressing the inevitability of people getting more or less what they deserve, and the fact that everyone has troubles, we read: "Now grief doesn't just grow out of the earth, nor trouble sprout from the dust. Because man is born for trouble, wbny ršp ygbyhw ʿwp. This phrase in the RSV is "as the sparks fly upward," in the Jerusalem Bible, "as surely as eagles fly to the height." Both these renderings suppose that the trope expresses inevitability--"man is born for trouble just as sure as. . . ." M. Pope in the Anchor Bible has "Man, indeed, is born for trouble, and Reshef's sons wing high"--noncommital, as he notes, but he suggests that "the sons of Rešep" might be flames, sparks or possibly various forms of pestilence.[310]

Caquot[311] again suggests that the bny ršp are winged demons. He concludes, "l'homme est né pour souffrir et le malheur vient, non pas de la terre, mais des démons qui volent dans le ciel hors de l'atteinte des hommes qu'ils ac-

---

reading en pedîlois hoi pódes autoû, "his feet are in sandals,"--which makes little sense. There are many divergences between MT and LXX in Hab 3. The Latin and Greek versions show many variations; ršp is alternately sermo (following LXX lógos), mors, pestis, volucer, volatile, ptēnón, ptôsis, and órneon. (See Vattioni, 67). The Targum has "an angel of death," the Peshitta simple "death." The Vulgate has "ante faciem eius ibit mors et egredietur diabolus ante pedes eius," which is more susceptible of Vattioni's and Caquot's interpretation.

309 P. Miller, The Divine Warrior in Early Israel (Cambridge, 1973), 118-119.

310 Once more the ancient versions seem to prefer a bird of some sort as the equivalent of Rešep, probably because of the presence of yagbîhû ʿûp in the sentence. It is likely that this interpretation of Job 5:7 was by extension largely responsible for the "bird" translations in the various ancient versions of the other OT passages where Rešep occurs. Albright (Studies for Paul Haupt, 150), noting that some ancient versions use gupós, "vulture," cites the familiar image of the vulture flying ominously over the dead, waiting for carrion. He sees vultures as appropriate "sons of pestilence." He rejects the translation "sparks" (based on the supposed "flame" connotation of a root *RŠP). This translation seems to be influenced by various early interpretations of Cant 8:6. See comments of Caquot, Semitica 6 (1956), 60, and Vattioni, 69.

311 Caquot, Semitica 6 (1956), 60.

cablent." Although he does not pursue the image, one might refer to the texts where Nergal sends diseases and plagues up from the underworld to bring man down. If the author of Job had some such thing in mind, the sense of the text might well be, "trouble doesn't just come from the earth; no, man is faced with preternatural powers, evil spirits always ready to rise up from the underworld to assail him--that's how inevitable trouble is."

Ps 91:5-6 offers a striking parallel:

"You will not fear the terror of the night,
nor the arrow that flies (ḥṣ yʿwp) by day;
nor the pestilence (dbr) that stalks in the darkness,
nor the destruction (qṭb) that wastes at noonday."

Dahood[312] suggests that Ps 91:5-6 clearly contains remnants of demonological terminology. With the presence of dbr and qṭb, it is hard to believe that ḥṣ yʿwp is not ultimately a reference to Rešep.

Ps 78:48 has another allusion to Rešep. In a list of evils God wrought against the Egyptians, "He gave their cattle over to brd, their flocks to (the) ršpym." Symmachus, however, reads dbr for brd, i.e., "plague."[313] Albright,[314] Caquot[315] and the translators of the Jerusalem Bible also read dbr, thence achieving a nice Deber/Rešep juxtaposition. The suggestion that brd itself might be yet another demon has not met with much acceptance.[316]

Simply from context it seems far more likely that God afflicted the animals with plague and diseases than with hail and lightening or thunderbolts. The allusion, after all, is to the plagues in Egypt. Although there was a plague of hail, the one specifically against animals was a dbr kbd mʾd (Ex 9:3ff.). I opt for the reading dbr over brd, translating as Deber and Rešeps, i.e., malevolent spirits accompanying God in his destructive wake, especially since the next verse

312 Dahood, in Anchor Bible, Psalms II (Garden City, N.Y., 1968), 332.

313 LXX has chấlazan/pyrí, "hail/fire." Most of the versions have something similar.

314 Albright, in Studies for Paul Haupt, 149. He suggests dittography with dābār in the next line.

315 Caquot, Semitica 6 (1956), 61.

316 Originally suggested by Nicolski in BZAW 46 (1927), 18. See comments of Vattioni, 72, and Caquot, Semitica 6 (1956), 61.

(49) says explicitly: "He loosed on them his blazing rage, wrath, indignation and distress, an escort of angels of evil (mšlḥt ml'ky rʿym)."

Ps 76:4 reads "(In Zion God) shattered the ršpy qšt, the shield, the sword, the weapons of war."[317] "Rešeps of the bow" seems to be a demythologization of the original image of Rešep. ršp(y) here apparently means little more than "vicious assault(s) (associated with bow and arrows)."

A similar demythologization of Rešep seems to occur in Cant 8:6 where we are told about love: ršpyh ršpy 'š šlhbtyh. Dahood[318] translates "A divine spark is its spark [taking ršpyh as ršp-yh, and the -y of ršpy as third person suffix, the latter of which suggestions is--in my view--both unnecessary and unlikely], its fire a divine flame [šlhbt-yh]." Other modern versions, although not so clever, convey the same general meaning.

Despite the fact that rešep(s) is evidently a common noun in this passage, its roots in mythology are unmistakable. Love is something like a demon--it grows and takes hold of the lovers, eventually beyond their control. Rešep(s) here, then, is more than flame(s). One can, for example, say in English that someone has been shot by the arrows of Cupid, where "Cupid" conjures up a more nuanced image than, say, "infatuation."

There remains, finally, to consider the Hebrew texts of Ben Sira 43, where ršp appears in v. 18 of both the Geniza and the Masada version, and should perhaps be restored in v. 13 of the Geniza version.[319] Chapter 43 of Ben Sira is an

317 The obscurity of ršpy-qšt is reflected in the ancient versions. LXX has tà krátē tôn tóxôn, "the powers of the bows," followed by the Vulgate, potentias arcuum. Symmachus has toûs oiônoùs, tà toxeúmata, "the eagles, the bows." Of the modern versions, RSV translates "flashing arrows," the Jerusalem Bible, "lightening-swift arrow" (or, in a note, "flashings of bow"). Dahood takes ršpy as accusative of means + 3rd pers. suf. -y. He translates "There with his thunderbolts he shattered the bow."

318 Dahood, in W. Ward, Ed., The Role of the Phoenicians in the Interaction of Mediterranean Civilizations (Beirut, 1968), 134.

319 See Anon, Ed., Facsimiles of the Fragments Hitherto Recovered of the Book of Ecclesiasticus in Hebrew (Oxford, 1901), Pl. 34 (B xlii, 24-xliii, 17b), line 16; and Pl. 35 (B xliii, 17c-xliii, 33), line 1. The text as printed in Vattioni, 70-71, has several errors, as does his LXX text. Also, Y. Yadin, The Ben Sira Scroll from Masada (Jerusalem, 1965), 44, lines 14, 17a, 17b, 17c. Note displacement of 17b.

account of the wonders of God's creation: the firmament, the sun, moon, stars, the rainbow. Vv. 14 and 17-18 are within a passage extolling the majesty of snow and storms. The approach of the atorm is described in terms of a theophany and each of its facets is linked with an action of God: he sends driving snows by his command, he amasses the clouds in his majesty, he shakes the mountains by his appearance. In other words, what begins as a description of God's cosmic wonders merges into the classical literary form of a theophany, and thus is much like Hab 3.

Rešep here seems to be halfway between the concept of a lesser divinity in Habakkuk and the almost total demythologization of Canticles. Rešep is a cosmic force of sorts, but because of the winds, etc., with which he/it is juxtaposed, seems to be less than personal.

Based largely on these OT passages, the notion that Rešep was a weather-god has taken hold in the critical literature. It is possible that this impression has been heightened by confusion between the so-called "Hadad-bronzes" and the "Rešep-bronzes." Because of this idea, ršp ḥṣ is frequently translated "Rešep of the lightening."[320] The fact is there is little in the OT passages or elsewhere to substantiate the view that Rešep is a weather-god. In those places where he is associated with meteorological phenomena, it is rather that he is part of Yahweh's military escort in a theophany, and theophanies typically involve dramatic disturbances in the weather.

On the whole, all of the OT passages seem to suggest that Rešep represents some more-or-less uncontrolled cosmic force, typically as a bringer of plague and sudden death, or at least of a seizure beyond control. Like Dionysus in Greek mythology he is a mysterious and dark power, and--in the case of love--ineluctable passion. What we observe in the OT are various degrees of demythologization of this force; sometimes Rešep is a personal figure bringing destruction, sometimes he/it is little more than a metaphor. But even as a metaphor the diverse connotations, when pushed back to their mytholo-

320 Recall that Simpson, BMMA 10 (1952), 185, in explaining the inscription on the Oriental Institute stele (E29), suggested "he who winds about (as a lightening-god or storm-god)" because he assumed Rešep was a weather-god. This is the way a concept takes root in the literature and feeds on itself as it moves away from the original evidence.

gical roots, are all quite consonant with the primitive notion of Rešep as a chthonic god, the lord of the underworld and therefore intimately involved with the powers of death, the minion of a superior deity when he appears with his host.

Chapter III: Conclusion and Summary

A. REŠEP'S NAME

Rešep's name has been variously vocalized in the critical literature. Albright[321] has consistently favored Rašap, pointing to the analogy of Hadad, Baᶜal, etc. He notes the modern Arsûf, "which can only stand for Phoenician *(A)rsôp for Rašap. Accented short a regularly becomes ó > ô in Phoenician."[322] He considers the vocalization Rešep to be without scientific basis.

Grdseloff[323] has made much of the spelling r-šp in the Egyptian inscription from Gebel Agg (E8). He suggested the pronunciation eršôp on the ground that the šp-sign [actually šsp in the New Kingdom, but soon reduced to šp in value] was represented by šôp in Coptic.

But first of all, the spelling r-šp instead of r-š-p must be regarded as fanciful, examples of which become frequent in Lat Egyptian.[324] Secondly, as Stadelmann[325] points out, Coptic ô is a reflex of Late Egyptian ā, so that in the Gebel Agg inscription šp [Coptic šôp] would have been pronounced šap. Stadelmann also disputes the possibility of giving hieroglyphic r the value of ᵉr.

Aside from the single deviation at Gebel Agg, Egyptian invariably writes the name r-š-p or r-š-p-w, the latter occuring slightly more than twice as often as the former. The spellings with r-š-p are concentrated during the reign of Amenophis II, but they also occur in the Ramesside and Ptolemaic times, so it is impossible to associate either spelling

321 Albright, AfO 7 (1931/32), 167.

322 Albright, as above. See also footnotes 185-187 of this study.

323 Grdseloff, Les débuts, 11ff. See also Thompson, MEKAL, 145.

324 See Leibovitch, ASAE 39 (1939), 156-157, and esp. Grdseloff, Les débuts, 12-15.

325 Stadelmann, Gottheiten, 47ff.

with a particular period.

It is likely that r-š-p reflects the Syrian pronunciation,[326] and that r-š-p-w is an Egyptianization in analogy to such divine names as Ḫnmw (Khnum), Ḫnšu (Khons), Mnw (Min), Mnṯw (Mont[u]), Šśmw (Sesem) and Śpdw (Sopd).

In Hebrew ršp takes the form of a segholate, i.e., rešep, pointing, of course, to an original rašp(u). This accords well with the Akkadian ra-ša-ap (Amorite ra-sa-ap) in the compound personal names, where the absolute state used for divine names in such an environment would suggest that the second -a- is merely an anaptyptic vowel, and that the original form is rašpu. Ru-uš-pa-an as an onomastic element in Akkadian seems to be a secondary formation. The Punic ʾršp and the Hurrian iršp do not necessarily suggest an original prothetic vowel as Grdseloff suggests, since both forms may be easily explained by phonetic developments peculiar to those two languages.

The evidence, then, would seem to indicate that the most primitive form was rašpu.[326a] Rašap is an expanded form with an anaptyptic vowel, as is the Hebrew rešep. There seems no good reason for abandoning Rešep as the usual English name for this god, despite Albright's antipathy to this form. It is impossible to vocalize the Egyptian with certainty. To suppose that r-š-p = rašap and that r-š-p-w = raš(a)pu is at least compatible with the evidence.

It has been usual to consider the name Rešep as a noun-form of a root *RŠP, to which the meaning "to burn" is generally attached. Thus Dahood:[327] "Within the purview of Northwest Semitic the etymology of Rešep is not difficult to establish. In biblical Hebrew the common noun rešep signifies 'pestilence, plague, flame' from the root RŠP "to burn," while in Aramaic rišpâ denotes 'flame.'"[328]

326 The fact that the earliest attested occurrence of Rešep in Egypt is in the name of an Asiatic and is spelled ršpw does not go against this view. Just as the gentleman in question was undoubtedly Egyptianized, so could his name have been.

326a See assembled evidence in Schretter, Alter Orient, 111-116.

327 Dahood in Moscati, Divinità, 85.

328 Similar views are expressed by Gese in Die Religionen Altsyriens, 141-142; Du Mesnil du Buisson, Études, 64-65; Albright, Archaeology and the Religion of Israel, 79, and others.

This does not at all seem to be the case, and that for two reasons. First of all the uses of RŠP can all be traced back to the god Rešep himself. The meaning of ršp in the OT, by way of demythologization, derived from the characteristics of the god. Secondly, there is little evidence in comparative Semitics to support Dahood's derivation. We do not determine that Rešep was a god of disease because ršp seems to mean "disease" or "pestilence" in certain OT passages; rather we know that ršp in the OT might well mean "pestilence, etc." precisely because the word is a metaphor with roots in the mythology of Rešep who was a god of pestilence.

Appeal to Late Hebrew and Aramaic is of no avail. A perusal of the entries in Jastro's Dictionary under rešep and Aramaic rišpâ show that the meanings of these words--"glow," "flame," "spark," "bird," "lightening," etc.--are all traced back to early commentaries on and versions of the OT passages, and occur precisely in rabbinic works discussing these passages.

Arabic rasafa, "to go in shackles," "to be moored," is not helpful, and Akkadian rašbu, "formidable," is certainly doubtful as a cognate.[329]

In short we are able to find no root *RŠP in use except where derived from the name of the god himself. Yet the word has the ring of a Semitic root. It is possible that RŠP is a specialized triliteralization of a primitive Afroasiatic biliteral root, formed precisely to name a god. There are, e.g., supposed examples of such a triliteral development in a set of B/PR/L roots, all of which mean "to divide," "to split." The third consonant can be infixed as well as suffixed or prefixed. If this were the case, ŚRP, "to burn," might well be a related root.[330] (Perhaps RPH, RPŠ, TRP, ṬRP and even RPP/RḤP should be investigated.)

B. REŠEP'S ICONOGRAPHY

Rešep's iconographic representations are exclusively of

329 See also von Soden, Grundriss der akkadischen Grammatik [= Analecta Orientalia 33] (Rome, 1952), § 88f; and Roberts, Earliest Semitic Pantheon, 48.

330 See remarks of Caquot, Semitica 6 (1956), 61, n. 1.

Egyptian provenance.[331] Details of his dress and certain of his weapons are characteristically foreign--specifically, Syrian--in appearance. He is, furthermore, sometimes associated with Asiatic gods and goddesses: ʿAnat,[332] ʿAstarte,[333] Šulman[334] and Ḥoron.[335] This would indicate that throughout his career in Egypt he was regarded for the most part as a foreign god, a "resident alien," to use Simpson's felicitous expression.[336]

Although Rešep is depicted on Egyptian stelae and mentioned in Egyptian texts from the time of the mid-Eighteenth Dynasty all the way into Ptolemaic times (with a geographical range from the Delta in the north to Nubia in the South), it was during the reign of Amenophis II and in the early Ramesside era that his cult seems to have had special prominence. During both these periods there is good reason to suppose peculiar Syrian influence: in the first instance, a certain Syrophile trend prevailed in official circles following conquests in Asia, with Amenophis adopting Rešep as his personal military god; in the second instance, there was a large influx of Syrian workmen into the Theban area, whence many of the Ramesside stelae emanate.

On most of the stelae, plaques and other objects Rešep assumes a warlike stance. He generally wears a short battle-kilt,[337] although he occasionally wears a fringed Asiatic kilt.[338] Once[339] he wears a long tunic. He usually brandishes a mace-axe over his head, although on occasion there is a different weapon.[340] In his other hand is most often a

331 I consider the so-called "Rešep-bronzes" too uncertain in their identification to be useful for Rešep's iconography.

332 The k3ḥ3 Stele (E38) and the Turin Altar (E50).

333 E3, E20, E49.

334 Aberdeen Stele, E13

335 Stele Cairo 86123, E19.

336 Simpson in Orientalia 29 (1960), 73.

337 E9, E10, E22, E23, E24, E39, E40, E47, E49.

338 E29, E32, E40, E30.

339 Gebel Agg, E8.

340 E18 (pole-axe), E22 (simple mace), E24 and E41 (a spear), E29 (fenestrated axe), E49 (knives?), E20 [Rešep?] (harpé).

spear and a shield; now and then one or the other is missing. On a few of the stelae either or both of the hands has no weapon at all, but rather a w3s-scepter or an ʿankh.[341]

On the Leibovitch Fragment (E22), the Scarab Strassburg (E31), the Brussels Fragment (E32) and the Stele Strassburg (E39) Rešep has a quiver on his back; there may be a quiver used as a symbol behind Rešep on the Seal Jerusalem (E16). These instances are noteworthy, since it has not generally been observed that arrows (or at least arrow-containers) are associated with Rešep in Egypt. This fact should be considered when interpreting ršp ḥṣ/ḥẓ in Northwest Semitic material.

His headgear is typically the high, conical Upper Egyptian crown. Slightly more than half the time this crown has a gazelle-head affixed to the front, and almost always it has one or two bands hanging down the back. Twice[342] the emblem in front is not a gazelle-head, but a uraeus, and once[343] the gazelle-head is not affixed to a crown, but tied around the head with a fillet.

Various symbols are found on Rešep stelae and scarabs, but aside from the unidentified banjo-like object[344] none of them seems especially significant

C. REŠEP'S EGYPTIAN EPITHETS

The most common epithet of Rešep on Egyptian stelae is simply nṯr ʿ3, "the great god," or nṯr ʿ3 nb pt, "the great god, lord of the sky." These are common Egyptian divine epithets and tell us nothing peculiar to Rešep.

On the Stele Berlin (E9) he is called ršpw nṯr ʿ3 sḏm nḥ, "Rešep, the great god, who hears prayer." In the Chester Beatty Papyrus (E21) he is "lord of the 3st," 3st being an unknown anatomical term, probably something in the (male) genital area. The context does not suggest in any way that Rešep is a god of fertility. In the rather esoteric Leiden

341 See E19, E34, E38, and E51 (if that is Rešep).

342 E23, E9.

343 E38.

344 E22, E23, E24.

Magical Papyrus (E26) in which many foreign gods are evoked in what seem to be fairly arbitrary roles, a disease is threatened with the "poisons of Rešep and his wife ỉtwm." ỉtwm cannot be identified. In a broken section of the same text, apparently an exorcism against a disease, we read "you shall go before those whom Rešep kills." Whether for good or for ill, Rešep is associated with disease and death in these passages.

The inscription on the Chicago Stele (E29) is problematic. "Rešep who winds about?/ gives increase? / draws near for battle?" On the Sai Relief (E11) Rešep seems to be "the encircler of the desert, who scorches."

The most elaborate epithets for Rešep are found on some of the Min-Qudšu-Rešep stelae, whereon all three gods have extraordinary titles. On Louvre 86 (E34) Rešep is "the great god, lord of eternity, sovereign everlasting, master mighty amidst the divine ennead (psdt)." On the Stele Turin (E36) he is "great god, lord of the sky, master of power, everlasting god." In both these instances the exalted titles given to Rešep seem due more to the enthusiasm of his devotees than to a particularly high place in the Theban pantheon for Rešep, for which there is little other evidence.

D. REŠEP IN EGYPT: THEMES

That Rešep was viewed as a warrior-god in Egypt is prima facie evident from his appearance on stelae. There is also literary evidence. On the Sphinx Stele (E3) Rešep and ʿAstarte are said to rejoice in Amenophis' prowess at horsemanship (in context viewed as preparation for his future role as a warrior), and in this text he is associated with Montu, the Egyptian war-god. Indeed, in an inscription in the Festival Building (E4) it is possible that Rešep and Montu are identified. On the Memphis Stele (E5) the pharaoh is said to storm over the Orontes (in battle) like Rešep. The parallel text has Montu for Rešep. In an inscription in the Mortuary Temple of Ramses III (E44) his soldiers are said to be "as mighty as Rešeps."

Some authors[345] have interpreted the juxtaposition of

345 E.g., Stadelmann, Gottheiten, 73ff.

Min, Qudšu and Rešep as evidence that Rešep was a fertility-god for the Egyptians, at least at Thebes in the Ramesside era. Although there is no doubt that Rešep was conceived of in a benevolent role on these stelae (and probably on some others), he is still for the most part portrayed as a warrior. I have interpreted this, largely since the stelae seem to be of directly Syrian inspiration, as a sign that his martial qualities were a "security umbrella" for Syrians in Egypt, and that his association with Qudšu and Min is not thematic.

E. REŠEP IN NORTHWEST SEMITIC MATERIAL

The early onomastica leave little doubt that Rešep is Amorite--or at least West Semitic--in origin.[346] There are many indications that the most primitive conception of Rešep in his Syrian homeland was as a god of the underworld, a chthonic deity intimately involved in the darker aspects of human life, especially in those things that lead to death. In this respect he is remarkably like the Mesopotamian Nergal, and at Ras Shamra, he is explicitly identified with him.

In the majority of contexts in which Rešep is to be found in Near Eastern texts, this basic image persists under a variety of epithets and descriptions. In the Ugaritic Keret story Rešep is responsible for the death of several of Keret's sons, evidently by plague. In one brief text (UT 143) Rešep seems to be receiving the sun into the underworld when her precipitous descent plunges the world into darkness.

In a Cypriot inscription and in a broken Ugaritic text Rešep is referred to as ršp ḥṣ and bʿl ḥẓ ršp respectively. In light of the fact that Rešep is repeatedly identified with Apollo at Cyprus, I have retained the idea that ḥṣ is arrow in the sense of "weapon" rather than of "luck." Apollo is a god who is said to spread disease and the plague through his arrows. It is also possible that solar associations also link Rešep with Apollo. Rešep probably = Apollo at Carthage.

In the OT Rešep has for the most part been demythologized. ršp is, in the OT, well on its way to becoming a common noun. Yet, in most contexts where ršp(m) occurs, it is not difficult to trace the literary trope back to its mythological roots where Rešep is an underworld god, a mysterious force assailing mankind with afflictions beyond his control. Thus in Hab 3:5 and in the Hebrew text of Ben Sira 43:17-18 he is a quasi-demon accompanying Yahweh in a theophany, causing a meteorological uproar. In Deut 32:23-24, Job 5:7, Ps 91:5-6 and Ps 78:48, he is a destructive force, bringing disease and disaster. Finally, in Cant 8:6 ršp(m) seems to be an uncontrollable force that turns even love into a consuming flame that will not be quenched.[346]

Rešep occurs as the divine element in many theophoric names, which fact would indicate that he could be viewed as a personal patron, a god with positive attributes vis-à-vis the individual involved. This positive side of Rešep is also attested in several of the Phoenician inscriptions where he appears as a patron of towns or of their rulers.

He is one of the patrons of Panammuwa and a special protector of Azitawadda. He is a popular god in Sidon, and even the Phoenician colony of Ibiza in Spain had a temple for him. Several cities in Cyprus had a special cult of Rešep-Apollo, and one inscription from Kition even speaks of a priest of Rešep.

As we have discussed in the Egyptian section of this study, some have suggested that the Near Eastern gods enjoy a certain polarity in their personalities, whereby they exhibit paradoxical characteristics: a god of disease and death such as Rešep would logically be invoked to withhold the sending of disease and death. But in fact Rešep is not invoked just to stay his hand (as he apparently is at least indirectly in the Leiden Papyrus [E26]). He is made a patron and worshipped for apparently rather positive reasons. Note, incidentally, that Nergal in Mesopotamia is also.

(It is needless to make much of this. This phenomenon is witnessed in a great number of mythologies. One has only to recall "classical" [and, alas, contemporary!] Satan-

346 This is an almost universal theme in world mythologies. Of the Greek Eros, for example, Cotrell (Concise Encyclopedia of Greek and Roman Mythology [Chicago, 1969], 103, says: "Eros . . . is accompanied by Pothos, longing, and Himeros, desire. Pothos and Himeros enter into the depths of the heart and incline it to love, casting aside all other concerns. In this way Eros often brings suffering and destruction upon human lives and men pray that they may be spared his visitations." The comparison I am implying here is not between Rešep and Eros, but between Rešep and the arrows of Eros.

worship, wherein Satan, as a destructive and death-bringing force is worshipped not only to avert evils, but also to bring about contact with secret world forces to control them for the purposes of the devotee.)

I have, in the course of this study, proposed that Rešep should not be thought of as a fertility-god, except insofar as he is a chthonic god, he is involved in general with the forces of life and death. To view him as being explicitly a fertility-god, however, seems to be an overinterpretation of the evidence.

I have also maintained that the view that Rešep is a weather-god is primarily a misunderstanding of the Old Testament passages in which *ršp* occurs, and to the subsequent misinterpretation of *ršp ḥṣ* as "Rešep of lightening."

Pl. I (E 18)

Pl. II (30)